THE

THE ORTHODOX FAITH

The Orthodox Faith series is intended to provide basic, comprehensive information on the faith and life of the Orthodox Church.
It consists of four volumes.

VOLUME I
Doctrine and Scripture

This volume is divided into two parts. The first outlines the doctrinal teachings of the Orthodox Church by looking at its sources, followed by a commentary on the Nicene Creed and an explanation of the doctrine of the Holy Trinity. Part two contains an explanation of the primary source of Christian doctrine—Scripture—through an overview of the contents of both the Old and New Testaments.

VOLUME 2
Worship

This volume contains five sections, highlighting different aspects related to worship in the Orthodox Church: the church building; vestments and symbols; the sacraments; the daily cycles of worship; the church year with its fasts and feasts; and the Divine Liturgy.

VOLUME 3
Church History

This volume summarizes the primary personalities, controversies, and events of the Christian era through a synopsis of each century, beginning from the birth of the Church through the early 21st century.

VOLUME 4
Spirituality

This volume deals with the main themes of Christian Life: prayer, fasting, repentance, the virtues, witness in the world, and communion with God.

THE ORTHODOX FAITH

Volume 1

DOCTRINE

and

SCRIPTURE

Thomas Hopko

With Illustrations by Andrew Tregubov

ORTHODOX CHURCH IN AMERICA

ST VLADIMIR'S SEMINARY PRESS

YONKERS, NY

The publication of this series was supported in part by a grant from the Ganister Orthodox Foundation Fund at the First Community Foundation Partnership of Pennsylvania.

ORTHODOX CHURCH in AMERICA

OCPC materials are published and distributed by

ST VLADIMIR'S SEMINARY PRESS
575 Scarsdale Rd, Yonkers, NY 10707
1–800–204–2665
www.svspress.com

ISBN 978–0–86642–079–2 (paper)
ISBN 978–0–86642–080–8 (electronic)

This second edition of The Orthodox Faith
is dedicated to the memory of the
Protopresbyter Thomas Hopko
(1939–2015)
"His soul shall dwell with the blessed"

CONTENTS

Preface

Some elders once visited Abba Anthony, and Abba Joseph was with them. The elder mentioned a verse from Scripture, wishing to put them to the test. He began to ask, starting with the least of them, what this verse was about and each one began to speak according to his own ability. But the elder said to each one: "You have not discovered it yet." Last of all he said to Abba Joseph: "You then, what do you say this phrase is about?" "I do not know," he replied—so Abba Anthony said: "Because he said, 'I do not know,' Abba Joseph has indeed discovered the way."

During the last years of his life, the late Protopresbyter Thomas Hopko was fond of carrying with him a copy of *The Arena,* by St Ignatius Brianchaninov, and a print-out of the thirty-eight sayings of St Anthony the Great from the *Alphabetical Sayings of the Desert Fathers,* from which the above quotation is taken. Being himself deeply rooted in the rich scriptural, patristic, and historical soil of the Orthodox faith, Fr Tom saw both texts as fundamental to the Christian life. He knew through his own experience what St Anthony was trying to convey to the elders that came to see him: that knowledge of God is best attained, not through study and discourse—though these have their place—but through the experience of living in Christ, which requires great humility and great love.

It is difficult to overestimate the importance of the series *The Orthodox Faith*, one of the earliest publications written by Fr Tom, the first volume of which came out in 1971. This deceptively labeled "elementary handbook" on the Orthodox Church has been used by thousands, from casual enquirers to catechumens to lifelong Church members, as both a catechesis and basic reference tool on Orthodox Christianity.

Yet the series has always been more than a simple set of reference manuals, precisely because it is the fruit of the living faith and understanding of tradition of its author, which give the work its sense of immediacy and zeal. Over forty-five years after their first appearance, these volumes continue to fulfill a dual purpose. First, they provide a rich base of introductory information on many aspects of Orthodoxy: Church doctrine and its development, Holy Scripture, liturgical practices, the spiritual life, etc. But, beyond this, through the rousing voice of Fr Tom, they remind us that our life in the Church—in Christ—means more than a vain repetition of ritual by a group of individuals.

Writing about the Liturgy, Fr Tom writes:

The Divine Liturgy is not an act of personal piety. It is not a prayer service. It is not merely one of the sacraments. The Divine Liturgy is the one common sacrament of the very being of the Church itself. It is the one sacramental manifestation of the essence of the Church as the Community of God in heaven and on earth. It is the one unique sacramental revelation of the Church as the mystical Body and Bride of Christ.

And so, it is more than fitting that these books be given an update in design and content after so many years of faithful service. Fr Tom had plans to revise and update all four volumes of this series. But alas, with his final illness and death in March, 2015, this was not to be.

Significantly, however, Fr Tom, working together with Dr David Ford of St Tikhon's Seminary, was able to complete one important piece of that plan, namely, a fully re-worked Church history volume. The revised and expanded Volume 3: *Church History* of this series contains the fruit of that labor, containing greatly enhanced coverage of major events in the history of the Church, from the Church's birth at Pentecost through the arrival of Orthodoxy to the Americas in the eighteenth century and into the early twenty-first. This new edition of *Church History* also includes theological and historical developments occurring in the West during the same periods.

Of course, in today's digital era, there are more considerations to take account of when updating content. These volumes will also be available for download in digital formats. Additionally, in an effort to provide more interactivity and the possibility for continual updates, the Department of Christian Education of the Orthodox Church in America has created a section on the OCA's website offering discussion questions and points for reflection. To view and download these resources as they become available, please visit: https://oca.org/orthodoxy/the-orthodox-faith.

My hope is that these volumes will continue to inspire those who have made use of them over the years and will serve as an introduction to the Orthodox Faith for a new generation of seekers and learners who are willing to enter into the experience of God by following the example provided by Protopresbyter Thomas Hopko and his words.

†Tikhon
Archbishop of Washington
Metropolitan of All America and Canada

PART I
DOCTRINE

1

SOURCES
of
CHRISTIAN
DOCTRINE

Revelation

Every morning at its Matins Service the Orthodox Church proclaims: "God is the Lord and has revealed Himself unto us; blessed is He who comes in the name of the Lord" (Ps 118.26–27). The first foundation of Christian doctrine is found in this biblical line: *God has revealed Himself to us.*

God has shown Himself to His creatures. He has not disclosed His very innermost being, for this innermost essence of God cannot be grasped by creatures. But God has truly shown what men can see and understand of His divine nature and will.

The fullness and perfection of God's self-revelation is found in His Son Jesus Christ, the fulfillment of the gradual and partial revelation of God in the Old Testament. Jesus is the one truly "blessed . . . who comes in the name of the Lord."

The first title given to Jesus by the people is that of **Rabbi**, which literally means **teacher**. In the English New Testament the word **Master** also issued in relation to Jesus in the sense of one who teaches, such as a schoolmaster or holder of a master's degree. Jesus' followers are also called **disciples**, which literally means students or pupils.

Jesus came to men first of all as the Teacher sent from God. He teaches the will of God and makes God known to men. He reveals fully—as fully as men can grasp—the mysteries of the Kingdom of God.

The coming of Jesus as teacher is one aspect of his being Christ the Messiah. The word **Christ** in Greek is the word for the Hebrew

Messiah which means the *Anointed of God*. For when the messiah would come, it was foretold, men would be "taught by God" (Is 54.13, Jn 6.45).

Jesus comes to men as the divine teacher. He claimed on many occasions that his words were those of God. He spoke as "one having authority" not like the normal Jewish teachers (Mt 7.29). And he accused those who rejected his teachings as rejecting God Himself.

> *He who believes in me, believes not in me but in him who sent me. And he who sees me sees Him who sent me. I have come as light into the world . . . for I have not spoken on my own authority; the Father who sent me has himself given me commandment what to speak. What I say, therefore, I say as the Father has bidden me* (Jn 12.44–50).

Jesus taught men not only by his words, but also by his actions; and indeed by his very own person. He referred to himself as the Truth (Jn 14.6) and as the Light (Jn 8.12). He showed himself not merely to be speaking God's words, but to be himself the Living **Word of God** in human flesh, the **Logos** who is eternal and uncreated, but who has become man as Jesus of Nazareth in order to make God known to the world.

> *In the beginning was the Word [Logos] and the Word was with God and the Word was God. He was in the beginning with God; all things were made through him, and without him was not any thing made that was made.*
>
> *In him was life and the life was the light of men. The light shines in the darkness, and the darkness has not overcome it.*
>
> *The true light that enlightens every man was coming into the world. He was in the world, and the world was made through him, yet the world knew him not.*

And the Word became flesh and dwelt among us, full of grace and truth; we have beheld his glory, glory as of the only-begotten Son from the Father.

And from his fullness have we all received, grace upon grace. For the law came through Moses; grace and truth came through Jesus Christ.

No one has ever seen God; the only-begotten Son who is in the bosom of the Father, he has made him known.

(See Jn 1.1–18; the Easter Liturgy Gospel Reading in the Orthodox Church.)

Jesus, the divine Word of God in human flesh, comes to teach men by his presence, his words and his deeds. His disciples are sent into the world to proclaim Him and His **Gospel**, which means literally the "glad tidings" or the "good news" of the Kingdom of God. Those whom Jesus sends are called the **apostles**, which means literally "those who are sent." The apostles are directly inspired by God's Holy Spirit, the Spirit of Truth (Jn 15.26), to "make disciples of all nations" teaching them what Christ has commanded (Mt 28.19).

The early Church, we are told, "devoted themselves to the apostles' doctrine" (Acts 2.42). **Doctrine** as a word simply means teaching or instruction. The apostles' doctrine is the doctrine of Jesus and becomes the doctrine of the Christian Church. It is received by the disciples of every age and generation as the very doctrine of God. It is proclaimed everywhere and always as the doctrine of eternal life through which all men and the whole world are enlightened and saved.

At this point it must be mentioned that although God's self-revelation in history through the chosen people of Israel—the revelation which culminates in the coming of Christ the Messiah—is of primary importance, it is also the doctrine of the Christian Church that all genuine strivings of men after the truth are fulfilled in Christ. Every genuine insight into the meaning of life finds its perfection in the

Christian Gospel. Thus, the holy fathers of the Church taught that the yearnings of pagan religions and the wisdom of many philosophers are also capable of serving to prepare men for the doctrines of Jesus and are indeed valid and genuine ways to the one Truth of God.

In this way Christians considered certain Greek philosophers to have been enlightened by God to serve the cause of Truth and to lead men to fullness of life in God since the Word and Wisdom of God is revealed to all men and is found in all men who in the purity of their minds and hearts have been inspired by the Divine Light, which enlightens every man who comes into this world. This Divine Light is the word of God, Jesus of Nazareth in human flesh, the perfection and fullness of God's self-revelation to the world.

It cannot be overstressed that divine revelation in the Old Testament, in the Church of the New Testament, in the lives of the saints, in the wisdom of the fathers, in the beauty of creation . . . and most fully and perfectly in Jesus Christ, the Son of God, is the revelation of God Himself. God has spoken. God has acted. God has manifested Himself and continues to manifest Himself in the lives of His people.

If we want to hear God's voice and see God's actions of self-revelation in the world, we must purify our minds and hearts from everything that is wicked and false. We must strive to love the truth, to love one another, and to love everything in God's good creation. According to the Orthodox faith, purification from falsehood and sin is the way to the knowledge of God. If we open ourselves to divine grace and purify ourselves from all evils, then it is certain that we will be able to interpret the scriptures properly and come into living communion with the true and living God who has revealed Himself and continues to reveal Himself to those who love Him.

Tradition

The ongoing life of God's People is called **Holy Tradition**. The Holy Tradition of the Old Testament is expressed in the Old Testamental part of the Bible and in the ongoing life of the People of Israel until the birth of Christ. This tradition is fulfilled, completed and transcended in the time of the Messiah and in the Christian Church.

The New Testamental or Christian Tradition is also called the **apostolic tradition** and the **tradition of the Church**. The central written part of this tradition is the New Testamental writings in the Bible. The gospels and the other writings of the apostolic church form the heart of the Christian tradition and are the main written source and inspiration of all that developed in later ages.

This Christian tradition is given over from people to people, through space and time. **Tradition** as a word means exactly this: it is that which is "passed on" and "given over" from one to another. **Holy Tradition** is, therefore, that which is passed on and given over within the Church from the time of Christ's apostles right down to the present day.

Although containing many written documents, Holy Tradition is not at all limited to what is written; it is not merely a body of literature. It is, on the contrary, the total life and experience of the entire Church transferred from place to place and from generation to generation. Tradition is the very life of the Church itself as it is inspired and guided by the Holy Spirit.

Not everything in the Church belongs to its Holy Tradition for not everything in the Church is done by the grace of the Holy Spirit, and not everything in the Church pertains essentially and necessarily to the Kingdom Of God. Some things in the Church are just temporal and temporary things, merely human customs and traditions of no eternal and everlasting value. Such things in themselves are not sinful or wrong. On the contrary, they may be very positive and very helpful to the life of the Church as long as they are not taken to be what they are not. Thus, it is very important in the Church to make the distinction between traditions which are merely earthly and human and passing away and the genuine Holy Tradition which pertains to the heavenly and eternal Kingdom of God.

It is also important to recognize that there are also things in the Church which not only do not belong to Holy Tradition, but which are not even to be counted among its positive human traditions. These things which are just sinful and wrong are brought into the life of the Church from the evil world. The Church in its human form, as an earthly institution, is not immune to the sins of its unholy members. These deviations and errors which creep into the life of the Church stand under the judgment and condemnation of the authentic and genuine Holy Tradition which comes from God.

Among the elements which make up the Holy Tradition of the Church, the **Bible** holds the first place. Next comes the Church's liturgical life and its prayer, then its dogmatic decisions and the acts of its approved churchly councils, the writings of the church fathers, the lives of the saints, the canon laws, and finally the iconographic tradition together with the other inspired forms of creative artistic expression such as music and architecture. All of the elements of Holy Tradition are organically linked together in real life. None of them stands alone. None may be separated or isolated from the other or from the wholeness of the life of the Church. All come alive in the actual living of the life of the Church in every age and generation, in every time and place. As the Church continues to live by the inspiration of the Holy Spirit, the Holy Tradition of the Church will continue to grow and develop. This process will go on until the establishment of the Kingdom of God at the end of the ages.

Bible

The written record of God's revelation is the **Bible**, which means the book, or the books. The Bible is also called the **Holy Scriptures**. Scripture as a word simply means writings.

The Bible was written over thousands of years by many different people. It is divided into two **testaments** or **covenants**. These words signify agreements, pacts, or we might say, "deals." The two basic covenants are the old and the new; each has its own scriptures. As a book, the Bible contains many different kinds of writings: law, prophecy, history, poetry, stories, aphorisms, prayers, letters and symbolical visions.

THE OLD TESTAMENT

The Old Testament scripture begins with the five books of the **Law** called the **Pentateuch**, which means the five books; also called the **Torah**, which means the Law. Sometimes these books are also called the **Books of Moses** since they are centered on the exodus and the Mosaic laws.

In the Old Testament there are also books of the history of Israel; books called the **Wisdom** books such as the Psalms, Proverbs, and the Book of Job; and books of the prophecies which carry the names of the Old Testament prophets. A **prophet** is one who speaks the Word of God by direct divine inspiration. Only secondarily does the word prophet mean one who foretells the future.

The Orthodox Church also numbers among the genuine books of the Old Testament the so-called **apocryphal** books, meaning literally the secret or hidden writings. Other Christians put these books in a secondary place or reject completely their being of divine inspiration.

THE NEW TESTAMENT

The center of the New Testament part of the Bible is the four **gospels** of Matthew, Mark, Luke, and John, who are called the four **evangelists**, which means those who wrote the gospels. Gospel in Greek is *evangelion* which means the "glad tidings" or the "good news."

In the New Testament scripture there is also the book of the **Acts of the Apostles**, written by St Luke. There are fourteen letters called the **epistles** (which simply means letters) of the Apostle Paul, though perhaps some, such as the **Letter to the Hebrews**, were not written directly by him. Three letters are also ascribed to the apostle John; two to the apostle Peter; and one each to the apostles James and Jude. Finally there is the **Book of Revelation**, also called the **Apocalypse**, which is ascribed to St John as well.

For the Orthodox, the Bible is the main written source of divine doctrine since God Himself inspired its writing by His Holy Spirit (see 2 Tim 3.16 and 2 Pet 1.20). This is the doctrine of the inspiration of the Bible, namely that men inspired by God wrote the words which are truly their own human words—all words are human!—but which nevertheless may be called all together the Word of God. Thus, the Bible is the Word of God in written form because it contains not merely the thoughts and experiences of men, but the very self-revelation of God.

The center of the Bible as the written Word of God in human form is the person of the Living Word of God in human form, Jesus Christ. All parts of the Bible are interpreted in the Orthodox Church in the light of Christ since everything in the Bible leads up to Christ and speaks about Him (Lk 24.44). This fact is symbolized in the Orthodox Church by the fact that only the book of the four gospels is enthroned on the altars of our churches and not the entire Bible. This is so because everything in the Bible is fulfilled in Christ.

The Liturgy

When the Church, which means literally the gathering or assembly of people who are called together to perform a specific task, assembles as God's People to worship, this gathering is called the **liturgy** of the Church. As a word, liturgy means the *common work* or action of a particular group of people for the sake of all. Thus the divine liturgy of the Christian Church means the common work of God done by the people of God.

The liturgy of the Old Testament people was the official worship in the temple of Jerusalem according to the Mosaic Law, as well as the annual feasts and fasts and the private prayers and services held by the Israelites at home or in the synagogues. **Synagogues** by definition are houses of gathering; they are not temples since, according to the Law, there was just the one **temple** in Jerusalem where the priestly worship was conducted. In the synagogues the Israelites gathered for prayer and scriptural study, preaching, and contemplation of the Word of God.

In the New Testament Church the liturgy is centered in the person of Christ and is primarily a "christening" of the Old Testament liturgical life. The Christian Church retains the liturgical life of the Old Testament in a new and eternal perspective. Thus, the prayers of the Old Testament, the scriptures and the psalms, are read and sung in the light of Christ. The sacrifice of the Body and Blood of Christ

replaces the Old Testament sacrifices in the temple. And the Lord's
Day, Sunday, replaces the old Jewish sabbath which is Saturday.

The Jewish feasts also take on new meaning in the Christian
Church, with the central feast of Passover, for example, becoming the
celebration of Christ's death and resurrection; and the feast of Pentecost becoming the celebration of the coming of the Holy Spirit, which
fulfills the Old Testamental Law. The Christian liturgical year is also
patterned after the Old Testamental prototype.

From the basic foundation of the Old Testament liturgy, the
Church developed its own sacramental life with baptism in the name
of the Holy Trinity, chrismation, holy communion, marriage, repentance, healing, and the Churchly ministry and priesthood taking on
specifically Christian forms and meaning. In addition, a great wealth
of specifically Christian prayers, hymns, and blessings were developed,
together with specifically Christian feasts and celebrations in remembrance of New Testamental events and saints.

The living experience of the Christian sacramental and liturgical
life is a primary source of Christian doctrine. In the liturgy of the
Church, the Bible and the Holy Tradition come alive and are given
to the living experience of the Christian people. Thus, through prayer
and sacramental worship, men are "taught by God" as it was predicted
for the messianic age (Jn 6.45).

In addition to the living experience of the liturgy, the texts of the
services and sacraments provide a written source of doctrine in that
they may be studied and contemplated by one who desires an understanding of Christian teachings. According to the common opinion
of the Orthodox Church, the sacramental and liturgical texts—the
hymns, blessings, prayers, symbols, and rituals—contain no formal
errors or deformations of the Christian faith and can be trusted absolutely to reveal the genuine doctrine of the Orthodox Church. It may
well be that some of the historical information contained in church
feasts is inaccurate or merely symbolical, but there is no question in

the Church that the doctrinal and spiritual meaning of all of the feasts is genuine and authentic and provides true experience and knowledge of God.

The Councils

As the Church progressed through history it was faced with many difficult decisions. The Church always settled difficulties and made decisions by reaching a consensus of opinion among all the believers inspired by God who were led by their appointed leaders, first the apostles and then the bishops.

The first church council in history was held in the apostolic church to decide the conditions under which the gentiles, that is, the non-Jews, could enter the Christian Church (see Acts 15). From that time on, all through history councils were held on every level of church life to make important decisions. Bishops met regularly with their priests, also called presbyters or elders, and people. It became the practice, and even the law, very early in church history that bishops in given regions should meet in councils held on a regular basis.

At times in church history, councils of all of the bishops in the church were called. All the bishops were not able to attend these councils, of course, and not all such councils were automatically approved and accepted by the Church in its Holy Tradition. In the Orthodox Church only seven such councils, some of which were actually quite small in terms of the number of bishops attending, have received the universal approval of the entire Church in all times and places. These councils have been termed the **Seven Ecumenical Councils** (see table below).

The dogmatic definitions (**dogma** means official teaching) and the canon laws of the ecumenical councils are understood to be inspired by God and to be expressive of His will for men. Thus, they are essential sources of Orthodox Christian doctrine.

Besides the seven ecumenical councils, there are other local church councils whose decisions have also received the approval of all Orthodox Churches in the world, and so are considered to be genuine expressions of the Orthodox faith and life. The decisions of these councils are mostly of a moral or structural character. Nevertheless, they too reveal the teaching of the Orthodox Church.

The Seven Ecumenical Councils

Nicea I	325	Formulated the First Part of the Creed, defining the divinity of the Son of God
Constantinople I	381	Formulated the Second Part of the Creed, defining the divinity of the Holy Spirit
Ephesus	431	Defined Christ as the Incarnate Word of God and Mary as Theotokos
Chalcedon	451	Defined Christ as Perfect God and Perfect Man in One Person
Constantinople II	553	Reconfirmed the Doctrines of the Trinity and of Christ
Constantinople III	680	Affirmed the True Humanity of Jesus by insisting upon the reality of His human will and action
Nicea II	787	Affirmed the propriety of icons as genuine expressions of the Christian Faith

The Fathers

There are in the Church a number of saints who were theologians and spiritual teachers who defended and explained the doctrines of the Christian Faith. These saints are called the **holy fathers** of the Church and their teachings are called the **patristic teachings** (*patristic* is from the Greek word for *father*).

Some of the holy fathers are called **apologists** because they defended the Christian teachings against those outside the Church who ridiculed the faith. Their writings are called **apologies** which means "answers" or "defenses."

Others of the holy fathers defended the Christian faith against certain members of the Church who deformed the truth and life of Christianity by choosing certain parts of the Christian revelation and doctrine while denying other aspects. Those who deformed the Christian faith in this way and thereby destroyed the integrity of the Christian Church are called the heretics, and their doctrines are called heresies. By definition **heresy** means "choice," and a **heretic** is one who chooses what he wants according to his own ideas and opinions, selecting certain parts of the Christian Tradition while rejecting others. By his actions, a heretic not only destroys the fullness of the Christian truth but also divides the life of the Church and causes division in the community.

Generally speaking, the Orthodox tradition regards the teachers of heresies as not merely being mistaken or ignorant or misguided; it accuses them of being actively aware of their actions and therefore sinful. A person merely misguided or mistaken or teaching what he believes to be the truth without being challenged or opposed as to his possible errors is not considered to be a heretic in the true sense of the word. Many of the saints and even the holy fathers have elements in their teachings which Christians of later times have considered as being false or inaccurate. This, of course, does not make them heretics.

Not all of the holy fathers were defenders against falsehood or heresy. Some of them were simply the very positive teachers of the Christian faith, developing and explaining its meaning in a deeper and fuller way. Others were teachers of the spiritual life, giving instruction to the faithful about the meaning and method of communion with God through prayer and Christian living. Those teachers who concentrated on the struggle of spiritual life are called the **ascetical** fathers, **asceticism** being the exercise and training of the "spiritual athletes"; and those who concentrated on the way of spiritual communion with God are called the **mystical** fathers, **mysticism** being defined as the genuine, experiential union with the Divine.

All of the holy fathers, whether they are classified as theological, pastoral, ascetical or mystical gave their teachings from the sources of their own living Christian experience. They defended and described and explained the theological doctrines and ways of spiritual life from their own living knowledge of these realities. They blended together the brilliance of the intellect with the purity of the soul and the righteousness of life. This is what makes them the holy fathers of the Church.

The writings of the Church Fathers are not infallible, and it has even been said that in any given one of them some things could be found which could be questioned in the light of the fullness of the Tradition of the Church. Nevertheless, taken as a whole, the writings of the Fathers which are built upon the biblical and liturgical foundations of Christian faith and life have great authority within the Orthodox Church and are primary sources for the discovery of the Church's doctrine.

The writings of some of those fathers who have received the universal approval and praise of the Church through the ages are of particular importance, such as those of Ignatius of Antioch, Irenaeus of Lyons, Athanasius of Alexandria, Basil the Great, Gregory of Nyssa, Gregory the Theologian, John Chrysostom, Cyril of Alexandria, Cyril of Jerusalem, Maximus the Confessor, John of Damascus, Photius of Constantinople, and Gregory Palamas; and those of the ascetical and spiritual fathers such as Anthony of Egypt, Macarius of Egypt, John of the Ladder, Isaac of Syria, Ephraim of Syria, Simeon the New Theologian, and others.

Sometimes it is difficult for us to read the writings of the fathers of the Church since their problems were often complicated and their manner of writing very different in style from our own. Also most of the spiritual and ascetical writings are put in the monastic setting and have to be transposed in order to be understandable and usable to those of us who are not monks or nuns. Nevertheless, it is important to read the writings of the fathers directly. One should do so slowly, a little at a time, with careful thought and consideration and without making quick and capricious conclusions . . . the same way that one would read the Bible. Among the church fathers, Saint John Chrysostom's writings are very clear and direct and can be read by many with great profit if the proper care is given. Also the **Philokalia**—an anthology of spiritual writings—exists in English, at least in part, and with proper care, it can be helpful to a mature Christian in search of deeper insights into the spiritual life.

The Saints

The doctrine of the Church comes alive in the lives of the true believers, the **saints**. The saints are those who literally share the holiness of God. "Be holy, for I your God am holy" (Lev 11.44; 1 Pet 1.16). The lives of the saints bear witness to the authenticity and truth of the Christian gospel, the sure gift of God's holiness to men.

In the Church there are different classifications of saints. In addition to the holy fathers who are quite specifically glorified for their teaching, there are a number of classifications of the various types of holy people according to the particular aspects of their holiness.

Thus, there are the **apostles** who are sent to proclaim the Christian faith, the **evangelists** who specifically announce and even write down the gospels, the **prophets** who are directly inspired to speak God's word to men. There are the **confessors** who suffer for the faith and the **martyrs** who die for it. There are the so-called **"holy ones,"** the saints from among the monks and nuns; and the **"righteous,"** those from among the lay people.

In addition, the church service books have a special title for saints from among the ordained clergy and another special title for the holy rulers and statesmen. Also there is the strange classification of the **fools for Christ's sake.** These are they who through their total disregard for the things that people consider so necessary—clothes, food, money, houses, security, public reputation, etc.—have been able to witness without compromise to the Christian Gospel of the Kingdom of Heaven. They take their name from the sentence of the Apostle Paul: "We are fools for Christ's sake" (1 Cor 4.10; 3.18).

There are volumes on lives of the saints in the Orthodox tradition. They may be used very fruitfully for the discovery of the meaning of the Christian faith and life. In these "lives" the Christian vision of God, man, and the world stands out very clearly. Because these volumes were written down in times quite different from our own, it is necessary to read them carefully to distinguish the essential points from the artificial and sometimes even fanciful embellishments which are often contained in them. In the Middle Ages, for instance, it was customary to pattern the lives of saints after literary works of previous times and even to dress up the lives of the lesser known saints after the manner of earlier saints of the same type. It also was the custom to add many elements, particularly supernatural and miraculous events of the most extraordinary sort, to confirm the true holiness of the saint, to gain strength for his spiritual goodness and truth, and to foster imitation of his virtues in the lives of the hearers and readers. In many cases the miraculous is added to stress the ethical righteousness and innocence of the saint in the face of his detractors.

Generally speaking, it does not take much effort to distinguish the sound kernel of truth in the lives of the saints from the additions made in the spirit of piety and enthusiasm of the later periods; and the effort should be made to see the essential truth which the lives contain. Also, the fact that elements of a miraculous nature were added to the lives of saints during medieval times for the purposes of edification, entertainment, and even amusement should not lead to the conclusion that all things miraculous in the lives of the saints are invented for literary or moralizing purposes. Again, a careful reading of the lives of the saints will almost always reveal what is authentic and true in the realm of the miraculous. Also, the point has been rightly made that men can learn almost as much about the real meaning of Christianity from the **legends** of the saints produced within the tradition of the Church as from the authentic **lives** themselves.

Canons

There are canon laws of ecumenical councils, of provincial and local councils, and of individual church fathers which have been received by the entire Orthodox Church as normative for Christian doctrine and practice. As a word **canon** means literally *rule* or norm or measure of judging. In this sense the canon laws are not positive laws in the juridical sense and cannot be easily identified with laws as understood and operative in human jurisprudence.

The canons of the Church are distinguished first between those of a dogmatic or doctrinal nature and those of a practical, ethical, or structural character. They are then further distinguished between those which may be changed and altered and those which are unchangeable and may not be altered under any conditions.

The dogmatic canons are those council definitions which speak about an article of the Christian faith; for example, the nature and person of Jesus Christ. Although such canons may be explained and developed in new and different words, particularly as the Church Tradition grows and moves through time, their essential meaning remains eternal and unchanging.

Some canons of a moral and ethical character also belong to those which cannot be changed. These are the moral canons whose meaning is absolute and eternal and whose violation can in no way be justified. The canons which forbid the sale of Church sacraments are of this kind.

There are, in addition, canons of a quite practical nature which may be changed and which, in fact, have been changed in the course of the life of the Church. There are also those which may be changed but which remain in force since the Church has shown the desire to retain them. An example of the former type is the canon which requires the priests of the church to be ordained to office only after reaching thirty years of age. It might be said that although this type of canon remains normative and does set a certain ideal which theoretically may still be of value, the needs of the Church have led to its violation in actual life. The canon which requires that the bishops of the Church be unmarried is of the latter type.

It is not always clear which canons express essential marks of Christian life and which do not. There are often periods of controversy over certain canons as to their applicability in given times and conditions. These factors, however, should not lead the members of the Church to dismay or to the temptation either to enforce all canons blindly with identical force and value or to dismiss all the canons as meaningless and insignificant.

In the first place, the canons are "of the Church" and therefore cannot possibly be understood as "positive laws" in a juridical sense; secondly, the canons are certainly not exhaustive, and do not cover every possible aspect of Church faith and life; thirdly, the canons were produced for the most part in response to some particular dogmatic or moral question or deviation in the Church life and so usually bear the marks of some particular controversy in history which has conditioned not merely their particular formulation, but indeed their very existence.

Taken by themselves, the canon laws of the Church can be misleading and frustrating, and therefore superficial people will say "either enforce them all or discard them completely." But taken as a whole within the wholeness of Orthodox life—theological, historical, canonical, and spiritual—these canons do assume their proper place and purpose and show themselves to be a rich source for discovering the living Truth of God in the Church. In viewing the canons of the Church, the key factors are Christian knowledge and wisdom, which are borne from technical study and spiritual depth. There is no other "key" to their usage; and any other way would be according to the Orthodox faith both unorthodox and unchristian.

Church Art

The Orthodox Church has a rich tradition of iconography as well as other church arts: music, architecture, sculpture, needlework, poetry, etc. This artistic tradition is based on the Orthodox Christian doctrine of human creativity rooted in God's love for man and the world in creation.

Because man is created in the image and likeness of God, and because God so loved man and the world as to create, save, and glorify

them by His own coming in Christ and the Holy Spirit, the artistic expressions of man and the blessings and inspirations of God merge into a holy artistic creativity which truly expresses the deepest truths of the Christian vision of God, man, and nature.

The **icon** is Orthodoxy's highest artistic achievement. It is a gospel proclamation, a doctrinal teaching, and a spiritual inspiration in colors and lines.

The traditional Orthodox icon is not a holy picture. It is not a pictorial portrayal of some Christian saint or event in a "photocopy" way. It is, on the contrary, the expression of the eternal and divine reality, significance, and purpose of the given person or event depicted. In the gracious freedom of the divine inspiration, the icon depicts its subject as at the same time both human and yet "full of God," earthly and yet heavenly, physical and yet spiritual, "bearing the cross" and yet full of grace, light, peace, and joy.

In this way the icon expresses a deeper "realism" than that which would be shown in the simple reproduction of the physical externals of the historic person or happening. Thus, in their own unique way the various types of Orthodox icons, through their form and style and manner of depiction as well as through their actual contents and use in the Church, are an inexhaustible source of revelation of the Orthodox doctrine and faith.

Musical expression may be added to the icon as a source of discovering the Orthodox Christian worldview. Here, however, there is greater difficulty because of the loss in recent years of the liturgical and spiritual meaning of music in the Church. Just as the theological meaning of the traditional Orthodox icon is being rediscovered, so is the traditional doctrinal significance of Orthodox music. The process in the latter case, however, is much slower, much more difficult, and much less evident to the average person.

The traditional Orthodox architecture also expresses the doctrine of the Church, particularly in its emphasis on "God with us" and the complete communion of men and the world with God in Christ. The use of domed ceilings, the shape and layout of the buildings, the placing of the icons, the use of vestments, etc., all express the teachings of the Church. The traditional Orthodox church architecture and artwork are expressions of the Orthodox Christian doctrines of creation, salvation, and eternal life.

It is a very important spiritual exercise for Christians to study the holy icons and the hymns of the Church's liturgy. One can learn much about God and His gracious actions among men by a careful and prayerful contemplation of the artistic expressions of Church doctrine and life (see *Worship*).

2

the
SYMBOL
of
FAITH

Nicene Creed

The **Nicene Creed** should be called the **Nicene-Constantinopolitan** Creed since it was formally drawn up at the first ecumenical council in Nicea (325) and at the second ecumenical council in Constantinople (381).

The word **creed** comes from the Latin credo which means "I believe." In the Orthodox Church the creed is usually called **The Symbol of Faith** which means literally the "bringing together" and the "expression" or "confession" of the faith.

In the early Church there were many different forms of the Christian confession of faith; many different "creeds." These creeds were always used originally in relation to baptism. Before being baptized a person had to state what he believed. The earliest Christian creed was probably the simple confession of faith that Jesus is the Christ, i.e., the Messiah; and that the Christ is Lord. By publicly confessing this belief, the person could be baptized into Christ, dying and rising with Him into the New Life of the Kingdom of God in the name of the Father, and of the Son, and of the Holy Spirit.

As time passed different places had different credal statements, all professing the identical faith, yet using different forms and expressions, with different degrees of detail and emphasis. These credal forms usually became more detailed and elaborate in those areas where questions about the faith had arisen and heresies had developed.

In the fourth century a great controversy developed in Christendom about the nature of the **Son of God** (also called in the Scripture the Word or *Logos*). Some said that the Son of God is a creature like everything else made by God. Others contended that the Son of God is eternal, divine, and uncreated. Many councils met and made many statements of faith about the nature of the Son of God. The controversy raged throughout the entire Christian world.

It was the definition of the council which the Emperor Constantine called in the city of Nicea in the year 325 which was ultimately accepted by the Orthodox Church as the proper Symbol of Faith. This council is now called the first ecumenical council, and this is what it said:

We believe in one God, the Father Almighty, Maker of heaven and earth, and of all things visible and invisible. And in one Lord Jesus Christ, the Son of God, the only-begotten, begotten of the Father before all ages. Light of Light; true God of true God; begotten, not made; of one essence with the Father, by whom all things were made; who for us men and for our salvation came down from heaven, and was incarnate of the Holy Spirit and the Virgin Mary, and became man. And He was crucified for us under Pontius Pilate, and suffered, and was buried. And the third day He rose again, according to the Scriptures; and ascended into heaven, and sits at the right hand of the Father; and He shall come again with glory to judge the living and the dead; whose Kingdom shall have no end.

Following the controversy about the Son of God, the Divine Word, and essentially connected with it, was the dispute about the Holy Spirit. The following definition of the Council in Constantinople in 381, which has come to be known as the second ecumenical council was added to the Nicene statement:

And [we believe] in the Holy Spirit, the Lord, the Giver of Life, who proceeds from the Father; who with the Father and the Son together is worshipped and glorified; who spoke by the prophets. In one Holy, Catholic, and Apostolic Church. I acknowledge one baptism for the remission of sins. I look for the resurrection of the dead, and the life of the world to come. Amen.

This whole Symbol of Faith was ultimately adopted throughout the entire Church. It was put into the first person form "I believe" and used for the formal and official confession of faith made by a person (or his sponsor-godparent) at his baptism. It is also used as the formal statement of faith by a non-Orthodox Christian entering the communion of the Orthodox Church. In the same way the creed became part of the life of Orthodox Christians and an essential element of the Divine Liturgy of the Orthodox Church at which each person formally and officially accepts and renews his baptism and membership in the Church. Thus, the Symbol of Faith is the only part of the liturgy (repeated in another form just before Holy Communion) which is in the first person. All other songs and prayers of the liturgy are plural, beginning with "we". Only the credal statement begins with "I." This, as we shall see, is because faith is first personal, and only then corporate and communal.

To be an Orthodox Christian is to affirm the Orthodox Christian faith—not merely the words, but the essential meaning of the Nicene-Constantinopolitan symbol of faith. It means as well to affirm all that this statement implies, and all that has been expressly developed from it and built upon it in the history of the Orthodox Church over the centuries down to the present day.

Faith

I Believe . . .

Faith is the foundation of Christian life. It is the fundamental virtue of Abraham, the forefather of Israel and the Christian Church. "Abraham believed the Lord, and he counted it to him as righteousness" (Gen 15.6).

Jesus begins his ministry with the same command for faith.

Jesus came into Galilee, preaching the gospel of God and saying, "The time is fulfilled, the kingdom of God is at hand; repent and believe in the gospel" (Mk 1.15).

All through his life Jesus was calling for faith; faith in himself, faith in God his Father, faith in the Gospel, faith in the Kingdom of God. The fundamental condition of the Christian life is faith, for with faith come hope and love and every good work and every good gift and power of the Holy Spirit. This is the doctrine of Christ, the apostles, and the Church.

In the Scriptures faith is classically defined as "the assurance of things hoped for, the conviction of things not seen" (Heb 11.1).

There are basically two aspects to faith; one might even say two meanings of faith. The first is faith "in" someone or something, faith as the recognition of these persons or things as real, true, genuine, and valuable; for example, faith in God, in Christ, in the Holy Trinity, in the Church. The second is faith in the sense of trust or reliance. In this sense, for example, one would not merely believe in God, in his existence, goodness, and truth; but one would believe God, trust his word, rely upon his presence, depend securely and with conviction upon his promises. For Christians both types of faith are necessary. One must believe in certain things with mind, heart, and soul; and then live by them in the course of everyday life.

Faith is sometimes opposed to **reason**, and belief to **knowledge**. According to Orthodoxy, faith and reason, belief and knowledge, are indeed two different things. They are two different things, however, which always belong together and which may never be opposed to each other or separated from each other.

In the first place one cannot believe anything which he does not already somehow know. A person cannot possibly believe in something he knows nothing about. Secondly, what one believes in and trusts must be reasonable. If asked to believe in the divinity of a cow, or to place one's trust in a wooden idol, one would refuse on the basis that it is not reasonable to do so. Thus, faith must have its reasons, it must be built upon knowledge, it must never be blind. Thirdly, knowledge itself is often built upon faith. One cannot come to knowledge through absolute skepticism. If anything is known at all, it is because there exists a certain faith in man's knowing possibilities and a real trust that the objects of knowledge are really "showing themselves" and that the mind and the senses are not acting deceitfully. Also, in relation to almost all written words, particularly those which relate to history, the reader is called to an act of faith. He must believe that the author is telling the truth; and, therefore, he must have certain knowledge and certain reasons for giving his trust.

Very often it is only when one does give his trust and does believe something that one is able to "go further," so to speak, and to come finally to knowledge of his own and to the understanding of things he would never have understood before. It is true to say that certain things always remain obscure and meaningless unless they are viewed in the light of faith which then provides a way of explaining and understanding their existence and meaning. Thus, for example, the phenomena of suffering and death would be understood differently by one who believes in Christ than by one who believes in some other religion or philosophy or in none at all.

Faith is always personal. Each person must believe for himself. No one can believe for another. Many people may believe and trust the same things because of a unity of their knowledge, reason, experience and convictions. There can be a community of faith and a unity of faith. But this community and unity necessarily begins and rests upon the confession of personal faith.

For this reason the Symbol of Faith in the Orthodox Church—not only at baptisms and official rituals of joining the Church, but also in common prayers and in the Divine Liturgy—always remains in the first person. If we can pray, offer, sing, praise, ask, bless, rejoice, and commend ourselves and each other to God in the Church and as the Church, it is only because each one of us can say honestly, sincerely, and with prayerful conviction: "Lord, I believe . . ."—adding, as one

must, the words of the man in the gospel—". . . help thou my unbe-
lief" (Mk 9.24).

In order for our faith to be genuine, we must express it in everyday
life. We must act according to our faith and prove it by the goodness
and power of God acting in our lives. This does not mean that we
"tempt God" or "put God to the test" by doing foolish and unnecces-
sary things just for the sake of seeing if God will participate in our
foolishness. But it does mean that if we live by faith in our pursuit of
righteousness, we can demonstrate the fact that God will be with us,
helping and guiding us in every way.

For faith to grow and become stronger, it must be used. Each
person should live according to the measure of faith which he has,
however small, weak and imperfect it might be. By acting according
to one's faith, trust in God and the certitude of God's presence is
given, and with the help of God many things which were never before
imagined become possible.

God

One God, the Father Almighty . . .

The fundamental faith of the Christian Church is in the one true and
living God.

> *Hear, O Israel: the Lord our God is one God; and you shall love the
> Lord your God with all your heart, with all your soul and with all
> your might. And these words which I command you this day shall be
> placed upon your heart, and you shall teach them to your children,
> and you shall talk of them when you sit in your house, and when you
> walk by the way, and when you lie down and when you rise . . ."*
> (Deut 6.4–8).

These words from the Law of Moses are quoted by Christ as the first and greatest commandment (Mk 12.29). They follow upon the listing of the Ten Commandments which begin, "I am the Lord your God . . . you shall have no other gods besides me" (Deut 5.6–7).

The one Lord and God of Israel revealed to man the mystery of his name.

And Moses said ". . . if they ask me, 'What is his name?' what shall I say to them?"

God said to Moses, "I AM WHO I AM." And he said, "Say to the people of Israel, 'I AM has sent me to you.'"

God also said to Moses, "Say to the people of Israel, 'Yahweh, the God of your fathers, the God of Abraham, the God of Isaac, the God of Jacob has sent me to you: this is my name forever, and thus I am to be remembered throughout all generations'" (Ex 3.13–15).

God's name is **Yahweh** which means I AM WHO I AM; or I AM WHAT I AM; or I AM WILL BE WHAT I WILL BE; or simply I AM. He is the true and living God, the only God. He is faithful and true to his people. He reveals to them His divine and holy Word. He gives to them his divine and holy Spirit. He is called **Adonai**: the Lord; and his holy name of **Yahweh** is never mentioned by the people because of its awesome sacredness. Only the high priest, and only once a year, and only in the holy of holies of the Jerusalem Temple dared to utter the divine name of Yahweh. On all other occasions **Yahweh** is addressed as the Almighty Lord, as the Most High God, as the Lord God of Hosts.

According to the Scriptures and the experience of the saints of both the old and new testaments, **Yahweh** is absolutely **holy**. This means literally that He is absolutely different and unlike anything or anyone else that exists (**Holy** literally means totally separated, different, other).

According to the Biblical-Orthodox tradition, even to say that "God exists" must be qualified by the affirmation that He is so unique and so perfect that His existence cannot be compared to any other. In this sense God is "above existence" or "above being." Thus, there would be great reluctance according to Orthodox doctrine to say that God "is" as everything else "is" or that God is simply the "supreme being" in the same chain of "being" as everything else that is.

In this same sense the Orthodox doctrine holds that God's unity or oneness is also not merely equivalent to the mathematical or philosophical concept of "one"; nor is his life, goodness, wisdom, and all powers and virtues ascribed to Him merely equivalent to any idea, even the greatest idea, which man can have about such reality.

However, having warned about an overly-clear or overly-positivistic concept or idea of God, the Orthodox Church—on the basis of the living experience of God in the saints—still makes the following affirmations: God may certainly be said to exist perfectly and absolutely as the one who is perfect and absolute life, goodness, truth, love, wisdom, knowledge, unity, purity, joy, simplicity; the perfection and superperfection of everything that man knows as holy, true, and good. It is this very God who is confessed formally in the Liturgy of St John Chrysostom as ". . . God, ineffable, inconceivable, invisible, incomprehensible, ever-existing and eternally the same."

It is this God—the Yahweh of Israel—whom Jesus Christ has claimed to be His Father. God Almighty is known as "Father" through His son Jesus Christ. Jesus taught man to call the Almighty Lord God of Hosts by the title of Father. Before Jesus no one dared to pray to

God with the intimate name of Father. It was Jesus who said, "Pray then like this: Our Father who art in heaven . . ."

Jesus could call God **Father** because He is God's only-begotten Son. Christians can call God **Father** because through Christ they receive the Holy Spirit and become themselves sons of God.

> *For when the time had fully come, God sent forth His Son, born of woman, born under the Law, to redeem those under the law, so that we might receive adoption as sons [or, so that we all might be made sons]. And because you are sons, God has sent the Spirit of His Son into our hearts, crying "Abba! Father!" So through God you are no longer a slave but a son, and if a son then an heir [of the Kingdom of God]*
> (Gal 4.4–7, The Christmas Epistle
> Reading in the Orthodox Church)

Thus no man is naturally a son of God and no man can easily call God Father. We can only do so because of Christ and the gift of the Holy Spirit. And so we say in the Orthodox Divine Liturgy:

> *And make us worthy, O Master, that with boldness and without condemnation, we may dare to call upon Thee, the Heavenly God as Father and to say: Our Father, who art in heaven . . .*

In contemplating the revelation of God our Father in the life of His people in the Old Testament and in the life of the Church in the New Testament, certain attributes and properties of God can be grasped by men. First of all, it can be clearly seen that God is Love, and that in all of His actions in and toward the world, God the Father expresses His nature as Love through Christ and the Holy Spirit.

> *Beloved, let us love one another; for love is of God, and he who loves is born of God and knows God. He who does not love does not know God; for God is love.*

*In this the love of God was made manifest among us, that God sent
His only-begotten Son into the world, so that we might live through
Him. In this is love, not that we loved God, but that He loved us, and
sent His Son to be the expiation for our sins.*

*So we know and believe that love God has for us. God is love, and
he who abides in love abides in God, and God abides in him*

(1 Jn 4.7–16).

*. . . God's love has been poured into our hearts through the Holy Spirit
which has been given to us* (Rom 5.5).

Being the God who is Love, our Father in heaven does all that
He can for the life and salvation of man and the world. He does this
because He is merciful and kind, longsuffering and compassionate,
willing to forgive and to pardon man's sins so that man might share in
the life and love of God. These gracious attributes of God are recalled
in the scriptural psalmody normally chanted at the beginning of the
divine liturgy in the Church.

*Bless the Lord, O my soul! And forget not all His benefits! Who forgives
all your iniquity, who heals all your diseases! The Lord is compassionate and merciful, long suffering and of great goodness!* (Ps 103).

Creation

Maker of Heaven and Earth . . .

The Orthodox Church believes that God the Father is the "Creator of
Heaven and earth and of all things visible and invisible."

To **create** means to make out of nothing; to bring into existence
that which before did not exist; or, to quote the Liturgy of St John
Chrysostom once more: "to bring from non-existence into being."

The Orthodox doctrine of **creation** is that God has brought everything and everyone which exists from non-existence into being. The

Scriptural description of creation is given primarily in the first chapter of **Genesis**. The main doctrinal point about creation is that God alone is uncreated and ever-existing. Everything which exists besides God was created by Him. God, however, did not create everything individually and all at once, so to speak. He created the first foundations of existence, and then over periods of time (perhaps millions of years, see 2 Pet 3.8) this first foundation of existence-by the power which God had given to it—brought forth the other creatures of God:

> *Let the earth put forth vegetation . . . let the waters bring forth swarms of living creatures . . . let the earth bring forth living creatures according to their kinds . . .* (Gen 1.19, 20, 24)

Thus, although God is certainly the creator of everything. He acts gradually in time and by means of things previously made by Him to which He has given life-producing potencies and powers.

According to the Orthodox Faith, everything that God makes is "very good": the heavens, the earth, the plants, the animals, and finally man himself (Gen 1.31). God is pleased with creation and has made it for no other purpose than to participate in His own divine, uncreated existence and to live by His own divine "breath of life" (Gen 1.30; 2.7).

> *By the Word of the Lord*
> *the heavens were made,*
> *and all their host by the*
> *breath (or Spirit) of His mouth.*
> *He gathered the waters of the sea as in a bottle;*
> *He put the deeps in storehouses.*
> *Let all the earth fear the Lord,*
> *let all the inhabitants of the world*
> *stand in awe of Him!*
> *For He spoke, and it came to be*

He commanded, and it was made!

(Ps 33.6–9)

In the above-quoted verses as well as in the account of Genesis we must notice the presence and action of God's Word and God's Spirit. God the Father makes all that exists by means of His Divine Word—"for He spoke and it came to be"—and by His Divine Spirit who "moved upon the face of the waters" (Gen 1.2). We see already a glimpse of the Holy Trinity to be fully revealed in the New Testament when the Word becomes flesh and when the Holy Spirit comes personally to the disciples of Jesus on the day of Pentecost.

We must make special notice as well of the goodness of the created physical world. There is no dualism in Orthodox Christianity. There is no teaching that "spirit" is good and "matter" is bad, that "heaven" is good and the "earth" is evil. God loves His entire material creation with His eternal love and, as we shall see, when the physical creation is mined by sin He does everything in His power to save it.

Loving the whole of His good creation, God the Father dwells within the world that He has made because of His goodness and love for man. The omnipresence of God is one of the divine attributes of the Creator particularly stressed in Orthodox Christian teaching. This fact is directly affirmed in the prayer to the Spirit of God which is used as the opening prayer of Orthodox worship:

O Heavenly King, the Comforter, the Spirit of Truth, who art everywhere and fillest all things. Treasury of Blessings and Giver of Life! Come and abide in us. And cleanse us from every impurity. And save our souls, O Good One!

The fact that Christians pray: Our Father who art in heaven . . . (or, literally, "in the heavens") is also an affirmation of the fact that God is present everywhere, for wherever men move on the face of the earth, over the seas or in the air, the heavens surround them with the presence of God. The Lord Jesus Christ, in order to have men realize that the true God, His Father, is not bound to one or another particular place, as were the pagan gods, teaches men to pray to the Father "in the heavens." For the one true and living God is present to all, over all, embracing and encompassing all with His heavenly care and protection. The God who is "over all" is also "through all and in all" (Eph 4.5). By His Word and His Holy Spirit, God "fills all in all" (Eph 1.10, 23).

Thus, the Apostle Paul also proclaimed to the Athenians, that whether men realize it or not, "in Him we live and move and have our being," for "He is not far from each one of us" (Acts 17.27–28). It is this fact of God's omnipresence in His creation, and our own presence in and to Him, that is witnessed to so beautifully in Psalm 139:

> *Whither shall I go from Thy Spirit?*
> *Or whither shall I flee from Thy Presence?*
> *If I ascend to heaven, Thou art there!*
> *If I make my bed in Sheol, Thou art there*
> *If I take the wings of the morning and dwell in the uttermost parts*
> *   of the sea,*
> *even there Thy hand shall lead me, and Thy right hand shall hold*
> *   me.*
> *If I say, "Let only darkness cover me, and the light about me be*
> *   night,"*
> *even the darkness is not dark to Thee, the night is bright as the day;*
> *for darkness is as light with Thee!*

(Ps 139.7–12)

Angels and Evil Spirits

All things visible and invisible . . .

In addition to the visible, physical creation there is an invisible world created by God. The Bible sometimes calls it "the heavens" and other times refers to it as "above the heavens." Whatever its symbolical description in the Holy Scriptures, the invisible world is definitely not part of the physical, material universe. It does not exist in space; it has no physical dimensions. And so it cannot be located, and it has no "place" which can be "reached" by travel within the galaxies of the spatial, locatable "places" of the physically created universe.

However, the fact that the invisible, created world is purely spiritual and is not discoverable on a map of the created material spaces makes it no less real or truly existing. The invisible creation exists as different from the created material universe and, of course, as totally different from the uncreated, absolutely super-divine existence of the uncreated God.

Invisible created reality consists of the hosts of bodiless powers, generally—and somewhat incorrectly—called the angels.

ANGELS

Angels (which means literally "messengers") are, strictly speaking, but one rank of the incorporeal or **bodiless powers** of the invisible world.

According to Orthodox Scripture and Tradition there are nine ranks of bodiless powers or the **Hosts** (**Sabaoth** means literally "armies" or "choirs" or "ranks"). There are **angels, archangels, principalities, powers, virtues, dominions, thrones, cherubim,** and **seraphim.** The latter are described as offering continual adoration and glory to God with the incessant and ever-resounding cry of Holy! Holy! Holy! (Is 6.3; Rev 4.8). Those in the middle of the above listing are little-known to men while the angels and archangels are seen as the active workers, warriors, and messengers of Yahweh relative to this world. Thus, angels and archangels are seen to struggle against spiritual evil and to mediate between God and the world. They appear in various forms to men in both the Old and New Testaments as well as in the life of the Church. The angels are those who bring the power and presence of God and who are messengers of His word for the salvation of the world. The best-known of the angels are Gabriel (which means literally "man of God"), the bearer of the good news of Christ's birth (Dan 8.16; 9.21; Lk 1.19, 26), and Michael (which means literally "who is like God"), the chief warrior of the spiritual armies of God (Dan 11.13; 12.1; Jude 9; Rev 12.7).

Generally speaking the appearances of the bodiless powers to men are described in a physical way ("six-winged, many-eyed"; or in the "form of a man"). However, it must be clearly understood that these are merely symbolical descriptions. By nature and definition the angels have no bodies and no material properties of any sort. They are strictly spiritual beings.

EVIL SPIRITS

In addition to the created spiritual powers who do the will of God, there are, according to the Orthodox faith, those who rebel against Him and do evil. These are the demons or devils (which means literally those who "pull apart" and destroy) who are also known both in the Old and New Testaments as well as in the lives of the saints of the Church.

Satan (which means literally the enemy or the adversary) is one proper name for the devil, the leader of the evil spirits. He is identified in the serpent symbol of Gen 3 and as the tempter of both Job and Jesus (Job 1.6; Mk 1.33). He is labelled by Christ as a deceiver and liar, the "father of lies" (Jn 8.44) and the "prince of this world" (Jn 12.31; 14.30; 16.11). He has "fallen from heaven" together with his evil angels to do battle with God and his servants (Lk 10.18; Is 14.12). It is this same Satan who "entered Judas" to effect the betrayal and destruction of Christ (Lk 22.3).

The apostles of Christ and the saints of the Church knew from direct experience Satan's powers against man for Man's own destruction. They knew as well Satan's lack of power and his own ultimate destruction when man is with God, filled with the Holy Spirit of Christ. According to Orthodox doctrine there is no middle road between God and Satan. Ultimately, and at any given moment, man is either with God or the devil, serving one or the other.

The ultimate victory belongs to God and to those with Him. Satan and his hosts are finally destroyed. Without this recognition—and still more—the experience of this reality of the cosmic spiritual struggle (God and Satan, the good angels and the evil angels), one cannot truly be called an Orthodox Christian who sees and lives according to the deepest realities of life. Once again, however, it must be clearly noted that the devil is not a "red-suited gentleman" nor any other type of grossly-physical tempter. He is a subtle, intelligent spirit who acts mostly by deceit and hidden actions, having as his greatest victory man's disbelief in his existence and power. Thus, the devil attacks "head-on" only those whom he can deceive in no other way: Jesus and the greatest of the saints. For the greatest part of his warfare he is only too satisfied to remain concealed and to act by indirect methods and means.

> *Be sober, be watchful. Your adversary, the devil, prowls around like a roaring lion seeking someone to devour* (1 Pet 5.8).

> *Put on the whole armor of God, that you may be able to stand against the wiles of the devil. For we are not contending against flesh and blood, but against the principalities, against the powers, against the world rulers of this present darkness, against the spiritual hosts of wickedness in the heavenly places* (Eph 6.11–12).

Man

Man is God's special creature. He is the only one "created in the image and likeness of God" (Gen 1.26). He is created by God from the dust at the end of the process of creation (the "sixth day") and by the special will of God. He is made to breathe "the breath of life" (Gen 2.7), to know God, to have dominion over all that God has made.

God created humans as male and female (Gen. 1.27; 2.21) in order "to be fruitful and multiply" (Gen 1.28). Thus, according to Orthodox doctrine sexuality belongs to the creation which God calls "very good" (Gen 1.31), and in itself it is in no way sinful or perverse. It belongs to the very nature of humanity directly willed by God.

As the image of God, ruler over creation and co-creator with the Uncreated Maker, man has the task to "reflect" God in creation; to make His presence, His will and His powers spread throughout the universe; to transform all that exists into the paradise of God. In this sense man is definitely created for a destiny higher than the bodiless powers of heaven, the angels. This conviction is affirmed by Orthodox Christianity not only because of the Scriptural emphasis on man as made in God's image to rule creation, which is not said about angels; but it is also directly affirmed because it is written of Jesus Christ, Who is truly the perfect man and the Last Adam (1 Cor 15.45) that "God has highly exalted him and bestowed upon him the name which is above every name, that at the name of Jesus every knee should bow, in heaven and on earth and under the earth, and every tongue should confess that Jesus Christ is Lord, to the glory of God the Father" (Phil 2.10–11).

It follows from belief in Jesus that man is created for a life far superior to that of any creature, even the angels who glorify God and serve the cause of man's salvation. It is precisely this conviction which is affirmed when the Church hails Mary the Mother of Christ as "more honorable than the cherubim and beyond compare more glorious than the seraphim." For what is glorified as already accomplished in the human Mary is precisely what is expected and hoped for by all men "who hear the word of God and keep it" (Lk 11.28).

Thus we see the great dignity of man according to the Christian faith. We see man as the "most important" of God's creatures, the one for whom "all things visible and invisible" have been created by God.

It is the Orthodox doctrine that one can understand and appreciate what it means to be human only in the light of the full revelation of Jesus Christ. Being the Divine Word and Son of God in human flesh, Jesus reveals the real meaning of manhood. As the Perfect Man and the Last Adam, the "man from heaven," Jesus gives us the proper interpretation of the story of creation given in the book of Genesis. For as the Apostle Paul has written, Adam finds his significance as "the type (or figure) of the one who was to come," namely Jesus Christ (Rom 5.14).

Thus it is written, "The first man Adam became a living being"; the last Adam became a life-giving spirit. But it is not the spiritual which is first but the physical, and then the spiritual. The first man was from the earth, a man of dust; the second man (Christ) is from heaven . . . Just as we have borne the image of the man of dust, we shall also bear the image of the man of heaven (1 Cor 15.45–49).

According to Orthodox theology, to bear the image of God is to be like Christ, the uncreated Image of God, and to share in all of the spiritual attributes of divinity. It is, in the words of the holy fathers, to become by divine grace all that God Himself is by nature. If God is a free, spiritual, personal Being, so human beings, male and female, are to be the same. If God is so powerful and creative, having dominion over all creation, so human creatures, made in His image and according to His likeness, are also to exercise dominion in the world. If God exercises dominion and authority not by tyranny and oppression, but by loving kindness and service, so are His creatures to do likewise. If God Himself is love, mercy, compassion and care in all things, so must His creatures, made to be like Him, also be the same. And finally, if God lives forever in eternal life, never dying, but always existing in perfectly joyful and harmonious beauty and happiness with all of creation, so too are human beings made for everlasting life in joyful and harmonious communion with God and the whole of creation.

According to Orthodox doctrine, human being and life is never completed and finished in its development and growth because it is made in the image and according to the likeness of God. God's being and life are inexhaustible and boundless. As the Divine Archetype has no limits to His divinity, so the human image has no limits to its humanity, to what it can become by the grace of its Creator. Human nature, therefore, is created by God to grow and develop through participation in the nature of God for all eternity. Man is made to become ever more Godlike forever, even in the Kingdom of God at the end of this age, when Christ will come again in glory to raise the dead and give life to those who love Him.

Thus the holy fathers of the Orthodox faith taught that whatever stage of maturity and development man attains and achieves, whatever his power, wisdom, mercy, knowledge, love, there continually remains before him an infinity of ever-greater fullness of life in the most blessed Trinity to be participated in and lived. The fact that human nature progresses eternally in perfection within the nature of God constitutes the meaning of life for man, and remains forever the source of his joy and gladness for all eternity.

It must be mentioned at this point as well that according to Orthodox Christian doctrine, the fact that humans are created male and female is the direct will of God and is essential for proper human life and activity as reflective of God. In a word, human sexuality is a necessary element in human being and life as made in the image of God. This does not mean that there is any sort of sexuality in God, but it does mean that human life must be sexual—male and female—if it will be what God Himself has made it to be.

Man and woman, male and female, are created by God to live together in a union of being, life and love. The man is to be the leader in human activities, the one reflecting Christ as the new and perfect Adam. The woman is to be man's "**helpmeet**," the "mother of all living" (Gen 2.18; 3.20). Symbolized in the relationship of Mary and the Church, the New Eve, to Christ, the New Adam, as the one who inspires man's life and completes his being and fulfills his life, the woman is not man's instrument or tool. She is a person in her own right, a sharer of the nature of God, a necessary complement to man. There can be no man without woman—no Adam without Eve; just as there can be no woman without man. The two exist together in perfect communion and harmony for the fulfillment of human nature and life.

The differences between men and women are real and irreducible. They are not limited to biological or physical differences. They are rather different "modes of existence" within one and the same humanity; just as, we might say, the Son and the Holy Spirit are different "modes of existence" within one and the same divinity, together with God the Father. The male and female are to be in spiritual as well as bodily union. They are to express together, in one and the same humanity, all of the virtues and powers that belong to human nature as made in the image and according to the likeness of God. There are no virtues or powers that belong to man, and not to woman; nor to woman and not to man. All are called to spiritual perfection in truth and in love, indeed in all of the divine virtues of God given to His creatures.

The hostilities and competitions between man and woman that exist in the present world are not due to their respective "modes of existence" as created by God. They are due rather to sin. There should be no tyranny of men over women; no oppression, no servitude. Just as there should be no striving of women to be men, and to hold the male position in the order of creation. There should be rather a harmony and unity within the community of being with its natural created order and distinctions. The oneness of nature with the distinction of various modes of being within Divinity, the Most Holy Trinity. For in the Divinity of the Trinity itself there is a perfect unity of nature and being, with real distinctions between the Father and the Son and the Holy Spirit as to how each of the Divine Persons lives and expresses the common nature of God. There is an **order** in the Trinity. There is even a **hierarchy** if we do not take this term to mean some difference in nature between the Father, Son, and Holy Spirit, but merely the **way** in which the Divine Persons relate to one another and to man and the world. For in the Trinity itself the Father alone is the "source of divinity." The Son is the expression of the Father and is "subject" to Him. And the Holy Spirit, of one essence and fully equal with the Father and the Son, is the "third" Person who fulfills the will of the Father and the Son. The Three Divine Persons are perfectly equal. This is a dogma of the Church. But they are not the same, and there is an ordered relation between them in which there are "priorities" in being and acting which not only do not destroy the perfection and perfect unity of the Godhead, but even allow it and make it to be perfect and divine (see "The Holy Trinity," below). It is the Trinitarian Life of God which is the Divine Archetype and Pattern for the being and acting of male and female within the order of creation.

Sin

The word **sin** means literally "missing the mark." It means the failure to be what one should be and to do what one should do.

Originally man was made to be the created image of God, to live in union with God's divine life, and to rule over all creation. Man's failure in this task is his sin which has also been called his **fall**.

The "fall" of man means that man failed in his God-given vocation. This is the meaning of Gen 3. Man was seduced by evil (the serpent) into believing that he could be "like God" by his own will and effort.

In the Orthodox tradition the eating of the "tree of the knowledge of good and evil" is generally interpreted as man's actual taste of evil, his literal experience of evil as such. Sometimes, this eating is also interpreted (as by St Gregory the Theologian) as man's attempt to go beyond what was possible for him; his attempt to do that which was not yet within his power to realize.

Whatever the details of the various interpretations of the **Genesis** story, it is the clear doctrine of Orthodoxy that man has failed in his original vocation. He disobeyed God's command through pride, jealousy and the lack of humble gratitude to God by yielding to the temptation of Satan. Thus man sinned. He "missed the mark" of his calling. He transgressed the Law of God (see 1 Jn 3.4). And so he ruined both himself and the creation which he was given to care for and to cultivate. By his sin-and his sins—man brings himself and all creation under the rule of evil and death.

In the Bible and in Orthodox theology these elements always go together: sin, evil, the devil, suffering and death. There is never one without the other, and all are the common result of man's rebellion against God and his loss of communion with Him. This is the primary meaning of Genesis 3 and the chapters which follow until the calling of Abraham. Sin begets still more sin and even greater evil. It brings cosmic disharmony, the ultimate corruption and death of everyone and everything. Man still remains the created image of God—this cannot be changed—but he fails to keep his image pure and to retain the divine likeness. He defiles his humanity with evil, perverts it and deforms it so that it cannot be the pure reflection of God that it was meant to be. The world also remains good, indeed "very good," but it shares the sorry consequences of its created master's sin and suffers with him in mortal agony and corruption. Thus, through man's sin the whole world falls under the rule of Satan and "lies in wickedness" (1 Jn 5.19; see also Rom 5.12).

The Genesis story is the divinely-inspired description in symbolic terms of man's primordial and original possibilities and failures. It reveals that man's potency for eternal growth and development in God was turned instead into man's multiplication and cultivation of wickedness and his transformation of creation into the devil's princedom, a cosmic cemetery "groaning in travail" until saved once more by God (Rom 8.19–23). All the children of Adam, i.e. all who belong to the human race, share in this tragic fate. Even those born this very minute as images of God into a world essentially good are thrown immediately into a deathbound universe, ruled by the devil and filled with the wicked fruit of generations of his evil servants.

This is the fundamental message: man and the world need to be saved. God gives the promise of salvation from the very beginning, the promise which begins to be fulfilled in history in the person of Abraham, the father of Israel, the forefather of Christ.

> *And the Lord said . . . to Abram [later named Abraham] "I will make you a great nation . . . and by you all the families of the earth will be blessed* (Gen 12.3; also 22.15).

Abraham believed God; and from him came the people of Israel from whom, according to the flesh, came Jesus Christ the Saviour and Lord of Creation (see Lk 1.55, 73; Rom 4; Gal 3).

The entire history of the Old Testament finds its fulfillment in Jesus. All that happened to the chosen children of Abraham happened in view of the eventual and final destruction of sin and death by Christ. The covenants of God with Abraham, Isaac and Jacob (whose name was changed to Israel which means "the one who struggles with God); the twelve tribes of Israel; the story of Joseph; the passover, exodus and reception of God's Law by Moses; the entrance into the promised land by Joshua; the founding of Jerusalem and the building of the temple by David and Solomon; the judges, kings, prophets and priests; everything in the Old Testament history of God's chosen people finds its final purpose and meaning in the birth, life, death, resurrection, ascension and glorification of God's only Son Jesus the Messiah. He is the one who comes from the Father to save the people from their sins, to open their tombs and to grant eternal life to all creation.

Jesus Christ

And In One Lord Jesus Christ . . .

The fundamental confession of Christians about their Master is this: Jesus Christ is Lord. It begins in the gospel when Jesus himself asks his disciples who they think that He is:

> *But who do you say that I am? Simon Peter replied, "You are the Christ, the Son of the Living God"* (Mt 16.16).

Jesus is the Christ. This is the first act of faith which men must make about Him. At His birth, the child of Mary is given the name Jesus, which means literally Saviour (in Hebrew Joshua, the name also of Moses' successor who crossed the Jordan River and led the chosen people into the promised land). "You will call his name Jesus, for he will save his people from their sins" (Mt 1.21; Lk 1.31). It is this Jesus who is the **Christ**, which means the **Anointed**, the **Messiah** of Israel. Jesus is the Messiah, the one promised to the world through Abraham and his children.

But who is the Messiah? This is the second question, one also asked by Christ in the gospels—this time not to his disciples, but to those who were taunting him and trying to catch him in his words. "Who is the Messiah?" he asked them, not because they could answer or really wished to know, but in order to silence them and to begin the inauguration of "the hour" for which he had come: the hour of the world's salvation.

Now while the Pharisees were gathered together, Jesus asked them a question saying, "What do you think of the Christ [i.e., the Messiah]? Whose Son is he?

They said to him, "The Son of David."

He said to them, "How is it then that David, inspired by the Spirit, calls him Lord, saying The Lord said to my Lord, sit at my right hand till I put thy enemies under thy feet" (Ps 110). If David thus calls him Lord, how is he his son?"

And no one was able to answer him a word, nor from that day did anyone dare to ask him any more questions.

(Mt 22.41–46)

After Jesus' resurrection, inspired by the same Holy Spirit who inspired David, the apostles and all members of the Church understood the meaning of his words. Jesus is the Christ. And the Christ is the Lord. This is the mystery of Jesus Christ the Messiah, namely that He is the One and Only Lord, identified with the God Yahweh of the Old Testament.

We saw already how Yahweh was always called Adonai, the Lord, by the people of Israel. In the Greek Bible the very word Yahweh was not even written. Instead, where the word Yahweh was written in Hebrew, and where the Jews said Adonai, the Lord, the Greek Bible simply wrote **Kyrios—the Lord**. Thus, the Son of David, which was another way of saying the Messiah, is called **Kyrios**, the Lord.

For the Jews, and indeed for the first Christians, the term **Lord** was proper to God alone: "God is the Lord and has revealed Himself unto us" (Ps 11.8). This Lord and God is Yahweh; and it is Jesus the Messiah as well. For although Jesus claims that "the Father is greater than I" (Jn 14.28), he claims as well: "I and the Father are one" (Jn 10.30).

Believing in "One Lord Jesus Christ" is the prime confession of faith for which the first Christians were willing to die. For it is the confession which claims the identity of Jesus with the Most High God.

Son of God

The only-begotten Son of God . . .

Jesus is one with God as His only-begotten Son. This is the gospel proclamation formulated by the holy fathers of the Nicene Council in the following way:

> *. . . and in one Lord Jesus Christ, the only-begotten Son of God, begotten of the Father before all ages: Light of Light. True God of True God. Begotten not made. Of one essence with the Father. Through whom all things were made . . .*

These lines speak about the **Son of God**, also called the **Word** or Logos of God, before his birth in human flesh from the Virgin Mary in Bethlehem.

There is but one eternal Son of God. He is called the **Only-begotten**, which means the only one born of God the Father. **Begotten** as a word simply means born or generated.

The Son of God is born from the Father "before all ages"; that is, before creation, before the commencement of time. Time has its beginning in creation. God exists before time, in an eternally timeless existence without beginning or end.

Eternity as a word does not mean endless time. It means the condition of no time at all—no past or future, just a constant present. For God there is no past or future. For God, all is **now**.

In the eternal "now" of God, before the creation of the world, God the Father gave birth to his only-begotten Son in what can only be termed an eternal, timeless, always presently-existing generation. This means that although the Son is "begotten of the Father" and comes forth from the Father, his coming forth is eternal. Thus, there never was a "time" when there was no Son of God. This is specifically what the heretic Arius taught. It is the doctrine formally condemned by the first ecumenical council.

Although born of the Father and having his origin in Him, the only-begotten Son always existed, or rather more accurately always "exists" as uncreated, eternal and divine. Thus, the Gospel of St John says:

> *In the beginning was the Word [the Logos-Son], and the Word was with God, and the Word was God* (Jn 1.1).

As the eternally-born of God and always existing with the Father in the "timeless generation," the Son is truly "Light of Light, True God of True God." For God is Light and what is born of Him must be Light. And God is True God, and what is born of Him must be True God.

We know from the created order of things that what is born must be essentially the same as what gives birth. If one comes from the very being of another, one must be the very same thing. He cannot be essentially different. Thus, men give birth to men, and birds to birds, fish to fish, flowers to flowers.

If God, then, in the super-abundant fullness and perfection of His divine being gives birth to a Son, the Son must be the same as the Father in all things—except, of course, in the fact of his being the Son.

Thus, if the Father is divinely and eternally perfect, true, wise, good, loving, and all of the things that we know God is: "ineffable, inconceivable, invisible, ever-existing and eternally the same" (to quote this text of the Liturgy once more), then the Son must be all of these things as well. To think that what is born of God must be less than God, says one saint of the Church, is to dishonor to God.

The Son is "begotten not made, of one essence with the Father." "Begotten not made" may also be put "born and not created." Everything which exists besides God is created by Him: all things visible and invisible. But the Son of God is not a creature. He was not created by God or made by Him. He was born, begotten, generated from the very being and nature of the Father. It belongs to the very nature of God-to God as God—according to divine revelation as understood by the Orthodox, that God is an eternal Father by nature, and that He should always have with Him his eternal, uncreated Son.

It belongs to the very nature of God that He should be such a being if He is truly and perfectly divine. It belongs to God's very divine nature that He should not be eternally alone in his divinity, but that His very being as Love and Goodness should naturally "overflow itself" and "reproduce itself" in the generation of a divine Son: the "Son of His Love" as the Apostle Paul has called him (Col 1.13, inaccurately translated in English).

Thus, there is an abyss drawn between the created and the uncreated, between God and everything else which God has made out of nothing. The Son of God, born of the Father before all ages, is not created. He was not made out of nothing. He was eternally begotten from the divine being of the Father. He belongs "on the side of God."

Having been born and not made, the Son of God is what God is. The expression **of one essence** simply means this: what God the Father is, so also—is the Son of God. **Essence** is from the Latin word *esse* which means **to be**. The essence of a thing answers the question **What is it?** What the Father is, the Son is. The Father is divine, the Son is divine. The Father is eternal, the Son is eternal. The Father is uncreated, the Son is uncreated. The Father is God and the Son is God. This is what men confess when they say "the only-begotten Son of God . . . of one essence with the Father."

Being always with the Father, the Son is also one life, one will, one power and one action with Him. Whatever the Father is, the Son is; and so whatever the Father does, the Son does as well. The original act of God outside of His divine existence is the act of creation. The Father is creator of heaven and earth, of all things visible and invisible. And in the act of creation, as—we confess in the Symbol of Faith, the Son is the one by **whom all things were made**.

The Son acts in creation as the one who accomplishes the Father's will. The divine act of creation-and, indeed, every action toward the world in revelation, salvation, and glorification—is willed by the Father and accomplished by the Son (we will speak of the Holy Spirit below) in one identical divine action. Thus, we have the **Genesis** account of God creating through His divine word ("God said . . ."), and in the Gospel of St John the following specific revelation:

He [the Word-Son] was in the beginning with God [the Father]; all things were made through [or by] him and without him was not anything made that was made" (Jn 1.2–3).

This is the exact doctrine of the Apostle Paul as well:

. . . in him [the Son] all things were created, in heaven and on earth, visible and invisible, whether thrones or dominions or principalities or powers-all things were created through him and for him. He is before an things and in him all things hold together (Col 1.16–17).

Thus, the eternal Son of God is confessed as the one "by whom all things were made" (Heb 1.2; 2.10; Rom 11.36).

The Symbol of Faith continues: . . . Who for us men and for our salvation came down from heaven and was incarnate of the Holy Spirit and the Virgin Mary and became man . . .

The divine Son of God was born in human flesh for the salvation of the world. This is the central doctrine of the Orthodox Christian Faith; the entire life of Christians is built upon this fact.

The Symbol of Faith stresses that it is "for us men and for our salvation" that the Son of God has come. This is the most critical biblical doctrine, that "God so loved the world that He gave his only-begotten Son that whoever believes in Him should not perish but have everlasting life" (Jn 3.16, quoted at each Divine Liturgy of St John Chrysostom at the center of the eucharistic prayer).

Because of his perfect love, God sent forth his Son into the world. God knew in the very act of creation that to have a world at all would require the incarnation of his Son in human flesh. Incarnation as a word means "enfleshment" in the sense of taking on the wholeness of human nature, body and soul.

> And the Word became flesh and dwelt among us, full of grace and truth; we have beheld his glory, glory as the only-begotten Son of the Father. And from his fullness have we all received grace upon grace" (Jn 1.14–16).

... came down from heaven ...

The affirmation that the Son has "come down from heaven and was incarnate" does not mean that the Son is located somewhere "up there" in the universe and then descended onto the planet earth. That He came "down from heaven" is the Biblical way of saying that the Son of God came from the totally "other" divine existence of God, outside the bounds and limits of all space and time located within the created, physical universe. In general we must remember again the symbolical character of all of our words and affirmations about God.

The affirmation that the Son came "down from heaven" also should not be interpreted in the sense that before the incarnation the Son of God was totally absent from the world. The Son was always "in the world" for the "world was made through Him" (Jn 1.10). He was always present in the world for He is personally the life and the light of man (1 Jn 4).

As "created in the image and likeness of God," every man—just by being a man—is already a reflection of the divine Son, who is Himself the uncreated image of God (Col 1.15; Heb 1.3). Thus, the Son, or Word, or Image, or Radiance of God, as He is called in Scriptures, was always "in the world" by being always present in every of his "created images," not only as their creator, but also as the one whose very being all creatures are made to share and to reflect. Thus, in his incarnation, the Son comes personally to the world and becomes Himself a man. But even before the incarnation He was always in the world by the presence and power of his creative actions in his creatures, particularly in man.

In addition to this, it is also Orthodox doctrine that the manifestation of God to the saints of the Old Testament, the so-called **theophanies** (which means divine **manifestations**), were manifestations of the Father, by, through and in his Son or Logos. Thus, for example, the manifestations to Moses, Elias or Isaiah are mediated by God's divine and uncreated Son.

It is the Orthodox teaching as well that the Word of God which came to the Old Testament prophets and saints, and the very words of the Old Testament Law of Moses, which are called in Hebrew the "words" and not as we say in English, the "commandments", are also revelations of God by his Son, the Divine Word. Thus, for example, we have Old Testamental witness to the revelation of God's Word, such as that of the Prophet Isaiah, in almost the same personalistic form as is found in the Christian gospel:

For as the rain and the snow come down from heaven, and return not thither but water the earth, making it bring forth and sprout, giving seed to the sower and bread to the eater, so shall my word be that goes forth from my mouth; it shall not return to me empty, but it shall accomplish that which I propose, and prosper in the thing for which I sent it (Is 55.10–11).

Thus, before His personal birth of the Virgin Mary as the man Jesus, the divine Son and Word of God was in the world by His presence and action in creation, particularly in man. He was present and active; also in the theophanies to the Old Testament saints; and in the words of the law and the prophets, both oral and scriptural.

Incarnation

And He was incarnate of the Holy Spirit and the Virgin Mary and became man . . .

The divine Son of God was born as a man from the Virgin Mary by the power of the Holy Spirit (Mt 1; Lk 1). The Church teaches that the virgin birth is the fulfillment of Old Testament prophecy

(Is 7.14), and that it is as well the fulfillment of the longings of all men for salvation which are found in all religions and philosophies in human history. Only God can save the world. Man alone cannot do it because it is man himself who must be saved. Therefore, according to Orthodox doctrine, the virgin birth is necessary not at all because of a false idolization of virginity as such or because of a sinful repulsion to normal human sexuality. Nor is it necessary as some would contend to give "added weight" to the moral teachings of Jesus. The virgin birth is understood as a necessity because the one who is born must not be merely a man like all others needing salvation. The Saviour of the world cannot merely be one of the race of Adam born of the flesh like all of the others. He must be "not of this world" in order to save the world.

Jesus is born from the Virgin Mary because he is the divine Son of God, the Saviour of the world. It is the formal teaching of the Ortho-dox Church that Jesus is not a "mere man" like all other men. He is indeed a real man, a whole and perfectly complete man with a human mind, soul and body. But he is the man which the Son and Word of God has become. Thus, the Church formally confesses that Mary should properly be called **Theotokos**, which means literally "the one who gives birth to God." For the one born of Mary is, as the Orthodox Church sings at Christmas: ". . . he who from all eternity is God."

Today the Virgin gives birth to the Transcendent One, and the earth offers a cave to the Unapproachable One! Angels, with shepherds, glo-rify Him! The wise men journey with the star! Since for our sake the eternal God was born as a little child! (Kontakion of the Nativity)

Jesus of Nazareth is God, or, more accurately, the divine Son of God in human flesh. He is a true man in every way. He was born. He grew up in obedience to his parents. He increased in wisdom and stat-ure (Lk 2.51–52). He had a family life with "brethren" (Mk 2.31–34), who according to Orthodox doctrine were not children born of Mary who is confessed as "ever-virgin," but were either cousins or children of Joseph.

As a man Jesus experienced all normal and natural human experiences such as growth and development, ignorance and learning, hunger, thirst, fatigue, sorrow, pain, and disappointment. He also knew human temptation, suffering, and death. He took these things upon himself "for us men and for our salvation."

> *Since, therefore the children share in flesh and blood, he himself likewise partook of the same nature, that through death he might destroy him who has the power of death, that is, the devil, and deliver all those who through fear of death were subject to lifelong bondage. For surely it was not with angels that he is concerned but with the descendants of Abraham. Therefore he had to be made like his brethren in every respect . . . to make expiation for the sins of the people. For because he himself has suffered and been tempted, he is able to help those who are tempted* (Heb 2.9–18).

Christ has entered the world becoming like all men in all things except sin.

> *He committed no sin; no guile was found on his lips. When he was reviled, he did not revile in return; when he suffered, he did not threaten; but he trusted to him [God the Father] who judges justly* (1 Pet 2.22; Heb 4.15).

Jesus was tempted, but he did not sin. He was perfect in every way, absolutely obedient to God the Father; speaking His words, doing His works, and accomplishing His will. As a man, Jesus fulfilled his role perfectly as the Perfect Man, the new and final Adam. He did all things that man fails to do, being in everything the most perfect human response to the divine initiative of God toward creation. In this sense, the Son of God as man "recapitulated" the life of Adam, i.e., the entire human race, bringing man and his world back to God the

Father and allowing for a new beginning of life free from the power of sin, the devil, and death.

As the Saviour-Messiah, Christ fulfilled as well all of the prophecies and expectations of the Old Testament, fulfilling and crowning in final and absolute perfection all that was begun in Israel for human and cosmic salvation. Thus, Christ is the fulfillment of the promise to Abraham, the completion of the Law of Moses, the fulfillment of the prophets and Himself the Final Prophet, the King and the Teacher, the one Great High Priest of Salvation and the Perfect Sacrificial Victim, the New Passover and the Bestower of the Holy Spirit upon all creation.

It is in this role as Messiah-King of Israel and Saviour of the world that Christ insisted upon His identity with God the Father and called Himself the Way, the Truth, and the Life: the Resurrection and the Life, the Light of the World, the Bread of Life, the Door to the Sheepfold, the Good Shepherd, the Heavenly Son of Man, the Son of God, and God Himself, the **I AM** (Gospel of St John).

DEFENSE OF THE DOCTRINE OF INCARNATION

In the Orthodox Church the central fact of the Christian faith, that the Son of God has appeared on earth as a real man, born of the Virgin Mary in order to die and rise again to give life to the world, has been expressed and defended in many different ways. The first preaching and the first defense of the faith consisted in maintaining that Jesus of Nazareth is in truth the Messiah of Israel, and that the Messiah Himself—the Christ—is indeed truly Lord and God in human form. The first Christians, beginning with the apostles, had to insist on the fact that not only is Jesus truly the Christ and the Son of God, but that He has truly lived and died and risen from the dead in the flesh, as a true human being.

By this you know the Spirit of God: every spirit which confesses that Jesus Christ has come in the flesh is of God, and every spirit which does not confess Jesus is not of God (1 Jn 4.2).

For many deceivers have gone into the world, men who will not acknowledge the coming of Jesus Christ in the flesh . . . (2 Jn 7).

In the early years of the Christian faith, the defenders of the faith—the apologists and martyrs—had as their central witness and task the defense of the doctrine that Jesus, being the Son of God in human flesh, has lived on earth, has died, has been raised by the Father, and has been glorified as the only King and Lord and God of the world.

THE ECUMENICAL COUNCILS

In the third and fourth centuries attempts were made to teach that although Jesus is truly the incarnate Son and Word of God, that the Son and Word Himself is not fully and totally divine, but a creature—even the most exalted creature—but a creature made by God like everything else that was made. This was the teaching of the Arians. Against this teaching, the fathers, such as Athanasius of Alexandria, Basil the Great, his brother, Gregory of Nyssa, and Gregory the Theologian of Nazianzus defended the definition of faith of the first and second ecumenical councils which held that the Son and Word of God—incarnate in human form as Jesus of Nazareth, the Messiah—Christ of Israel—is not a creature, but is truly divine with the same divinity as God the Father and the Holy Spirit. This was the defense of the doctrine of the Holy Trinity which preserved for the Church of all ages the faith that Jesus is indeed the divine Son of God, of one essence with the Father and the Holy Spirit, one of the Holy Trinity.

At the same time, in the fourth century, it was also necessary for the Church to reject the teaching of a certain Appolinarius, who claimed that although Jesus was indeed the incarnate Son and Word of God, the incarnation consisted in the Word merely taking a human body and not the fullness of human nature. This was the doctrine that Jesus had no real human soul, no human mind, no human spirit, but that the divine Son of God, who exists eternally with the Father and the Spirit, merely dwelt in a human body, in human flesh, as in a temple. It is for this reason that every official doctrinal statement in the Orthodox Church, including all of the statements of the ecumenical councils, always insists that the Son of God became man of the Virgin Mary with a rational soul and body; in other words, that the Son of God really became human in the full meaning of the word and that Jesus Christ was and is a real human being, having and being everything that every human being has and is. This is nothing other than the teaching of the Gospels and the New Testament scriptures generally.

> *Since therefore the children share in flesh and blood, He Himself likewise partook of the same nature . . . [being] made like His brethren in every respect . . .* (Heb 2.14–17)

THE NESTORIAN CONTROVERSY

In the fifth century a long and difficult controversy developed over the true understanding of the person and nature of Jesus Christ. The third ecumenical council in Ephesus in 431, following the teaching of St Cyril of Alexandria, was most concerned to defend the fact that the One who was born of the Virgin Mary was no one other than the divine Son of God in human flesh. It was necessary to defend this fact most explicitly because some in the Church, following Nestorius, the bishop of Constantinople, were teaching that the Virgin Mary should not be called **Theotokos**—a term already used in the Church's theology—because it was claimed that the Virgin gave birth to the man Jesus whom the Son of God had become in the incarnation, and not to the Son Himself. In this view it was held that there is a division between the Son of God born in eternity from God the Father and the

Son of Man born from the Virgin in Bethlehem; and that although there is certainly a real "connection" between them, Mary merely gave birth to the man. As such, it was held, Mary could be called **Theotokos** only by some sort of symbolic and overly-pious stretching of

the word, but that it is rather dogmatically accurate to call her **Christotokos** (the one who gave birth to the **Messiah**) or **Anthropotokos** (the one who gave birth to the Man that the Son of God has become in the incarnation).

St Cyril of Alexandria and the fathers of the council in Ephesus rejected the Nestorian doctrine and claimed that the term **Theotokos** for the Virgin Mary is completely and totally accurate and must be retained if the Christian faith is to be properly confessed and the

Christian life properly lived. The term must be defended because there can be no division of any sort between the eternal Son and Word of God, begotten of the Father before all ages, and Jesus Christ, the Son of Mary. Mary's child is the eternal and divine Son of God. He—and no one else—was born of her as a child. He—and no one else—was incarnate in human flesh from her. He—and no one else—became man in the manger in Bethlehem. There can be no "connection" or "conjunction" between God's Son and Mary's Son because they are in fact one and the same person. God's Son was born of Mary. God's Son is divine; He is God. Therefore, Mary gave birth to God in the flesh, to God as a man. Therefore, Mary is truly **Theotokos**. The battle cry of St Cyril and the Council in Ephesus was just this: The Son of God and the Son of Man—one Son!

THE COUNCIL OF CHALCEDON

This teaching about Jesus Christ, the incarnate Son of God, was further elaborated and explained by the definition of the fourth ecumenical council in Chalcedon in 451. This was necessary because there was a tendency to stress the divine nature of Christ to such an extent that His true human nature was underplayed to the point almost of being rejected. At the fourth council the well-known formulation was made which says that Jesus Christ, the incarnate Son and Word of God is one person (or hypostasis) having two full and complete natures: human and divine. Inspired particularly by the letter of Saint Leo, the Pope of Rome, the fourth council insisted that Jesus is exactly what God the Father is in relation to His divinity. This was a direct reference to the Nicene Creed which claims that the Son of God is "of one essence with the Father," which simply means that what God the Father is, the Son is also: Light from Light, True God from True God. And the council insisted as well that in the incarnation the Son of God became exactly what all human beings are, confessing that Jesus Christ is also "of one essence" with all human beings in respect to His humanity. This doctrine was and is defended as teaching nothing other than the apostolic faith as recorded in the Gospels and the New Testament writings, for example, those of the Apostle Paul:

> . . . *though He was in the form of God, [Jesus] did not count equality with God a thing to be clung to, but emptied Himself, taking on the form of a servant, being found in the likeness of men. And being found in human form He humbled Himself and became obedient unto death, even death on a cross* (Phil 2.6–8; See also Heb 1–2, Jn 1).

The critical words in the definition of faith of the Council of Chalcedon are the following:

Following the holy fathers we teach with one voice that the Son of God and our Lord Jesus Christ is to be confessed as one and the same [Person], and He is perfect in Divinity and perfect in Humanity, true God and true Man, of a rational soul and [human] body consisting, of one essence with the Father as touching His Divinity and of one essence with us as touching His Humanity; made in all things like unto us, with the exception of sin only; begotten of His Father before all ages according to His Divinity: but in these last days, for us men and for our salvation, born [into the world] of the Virgin Mary, Theotokos, according to His Humanity. This one and the same Jesus Christ, the only-begotten Son [of God] must be confessed to be in two natures, without mixture and without change, without separation and without division [i.e., without fusing together Divinity and Humanity so that the proper characteristics of each are changed or lost; and also without separating them in such a way that there might be considered to be two Sons and not One Son only] and that without the distinction of natures being removed by such union, but rather that the peculiar property of each nature being preserved and being united in one Person and Hypostasis, not separated or divided into two persons, but one and the same Son and only begotten, God the Word, our Lord Jesus Christ, as the Prophets of old have spoken concerning Him [e.g., the Immanuel of Is 7.14], and as Jesus Christ has taught us, and as the Creed of the fathers has delivered to us.

A number of Christians did not accept the Council of Chalcedon and broke communion with those who did accept it. They did so because they thought that the council had in fact resurrected the wrong doctrine of Nestorius by insisting on the "two natures" after the incarnation, however strongly and firmly the "union" of the two natures was insisted upon. These Christians were called the **monophysites** (from the term meaning "one nature" after the incarnation), and they continue until today in separation from the Chalcedonian

Orthodox in the Coptic, Ethiopian and Armenian churches. Hopefully, one day, by God's grace, this dispute will be resolved and those who adhere to Chalcedon the Eastern Orthodox Christians, as well as the traditional Roman Catholics and Protestants—will come to a unity of faith with those who reject Chalcedon in regard to its explication of the union of the divine and the human in the one person of Christ our Lord. Whatever the future may hold by God's grace, however, it is still the firm teaching of the Orthodox Church that the Council of Chalcedon is in strict adherence with the anti-Nestorian doctrines of Saint Cyril and the third ecumenical council in Ephesus. The virtue of the fourth council, in the Orthodox view, is that it defines very clearly the fact that when the Son of God was born as a man from the Virgin Mary, Theotokos, He did not cease to be God or change in His Divinity, while becoming a complete and perfect man in His incarnate Humanity. For salvation itself requires the perfect union of Divinity and Humanity in the one Person of Jesus Christ; a union where God is God and Man is Man, and yet where the two become one in perfect unity: without fusion or change, and without division or separation.

EMPEROR JUSTINIAN AND THE 5TH ECUMENICAL COUNCIL

In the sixth century, the Byzantine Emperor Justinian wanted to reaffirm the fact that the followers of the council of Chalcedon really believed that Jesus Christ is the incarnate Son and Word of God, one of the Holy Trinity. He wanted to do this primarily to convince those who did not accept the fourth council that its definition did not reintroduce the error of Nestorius. To do this, the Emperor called the council now known as the fifth ecumenical council in Constantinople in 553 which further served to clarify the Orthodox position in regard to the person and action of Christ. The following are some of the key texts of this council:

> *If anyone understands the expression "one Person only of our Lord Jesus Christ" in this sense, that it is the union of many hypostases [or persons], and if he thus attempts to introduce into the mystery of Christ two hypostases or two persons, and after having introduced two persons speaks of one Person only in the sense of dignity, honor or worship . . . [and] shall calumniate the holy council of Chalcedon, pretending that it used this expression [one hypostasis and person] in this impious sense . . . let him be anathema.*
>
> *If anyone shall not call in a true acceptation . . . the holy, glorious and ever-virgin Mary, the Theotokos . . . believing that she bare only a simple man and that God the Word was not incarnate of her . . . [and] shall calumniate the holy synod of Chalcedon as though it has asserted the Virgin to be Theotokos according to the impious sense . . . let him be anathema.*
>
> *If anyone using the expression "in two natures" does not confess that our one Lord Jesus Christ has been revealed in the divinity and in the humanity, so as to designate by that expression a difference of the natures of which an ineffable union is made without confusion, in which neither the nature of the Word was changed into that of the flesh, nor that of the flesh into that of the Word, for each remained what it was by nature, the union being hypostatic [i.e., in the one Person]; but shall take the expression to divide the parties . . . let him be anathema.*
>
> *If anyone does not confess that our Lord Jesus Christ who was crucified in the flesh is true Gad and the Lord of Glory and one of the Holy Trinity, let him be anathema.*

To further emphasize the point that the Chalcedonian Council was truly orthodox, the Emperor Justinian wrote a doctrinal hymn which is still sung in the Orthodox Church at every divine liturgy. It confesses the Lord Jesus Christ as perfect God and perfect man.

> *Only-begotten Son and Word of God,*
> *Who for our salvation willed to be incarnate of*
> *the holy Theotokos and ever-virgin Mary,*
> *Who without change became man and was crucified,*
> *Who is one of the Holy Trinity, glorified with*
> *the Father and the Holy Spirit,*
> *O Christ our God, trampling down death by death,*
> *Save us!*

THE MONOTHELITE CONTROVERSY

In the seventh century the question of how to understand, define and confess the person and action of Jesus Christ continued to cause divisions among the believers. Some now said that after the Son of God became man, He had just one activity and will—the theandric activity and will of the Word-made—flesh. These people, called **monothelites**, insisted that the One Person of Christ, in uniting the natures of God and Man in His One Person, fused together the human and divine will and activity in such a way that they no longer could be distinguished.

The sixth ecumenical council met in Constantinople in 680–681. Following the teachings of St Maximus the Confessor who was imprisoned and tortured for his doctrines, it decreed that just as Christ is really fully divine and fully human, the perfect union of Divinity and Humanity in one Person, so also He must have both a real human activity and will and a real divine activity and will according to each of His natures and that these two wills and activities, like the natures themselves, should not be understood to be fused or mingled together into one so as to lose their proper natural characteristics and properties. This decision was based on the fact that since the Son of God remained fully divine in the incarnation, He must continue to have His proper divine activity and will; and that since He became fully human in the incarnation He must also have a complete and perfect human activity and will; and that the salvation of mankind requires that the distinction but not the division or separation of each of these respective activities and wills remain in the incarnate Saviour. The following is part of the definition of faith of the sixth council:

> . . . *in Him are two natural wills and two natural operations without division, without fusion, without change and without separation according to the teaching of the holy fathers. And these two natural wills are not contrary to one another (God forbid!) . . . but His human will follows, and not as resisting and reluctant, but rather as subject to His divine and omnipotent will . . . For as His most holy and immaculate animated flesh was not destroyed because it was deified but continued in its own state and nature, so also His human will, although deified, was not suppressed, but was rather preserved . . . We glorify two natural operations . . . in the same Lord Jesus Christ our true God, that is to say a divine operation [or action] and a human operation*

> . . . *For we will not admit one natural operation in God and in the creature. . . . believing our Lord Jesus Christ to be one of the Trinity, and after the incarnation our true God we say that His two natures shone forth in His one hypostasis [or person] in which He both performed the miracles and endured the sufferings . . . Wherefore we confess two wills and two operations concurring most fitly in Him for the salvation of the human race.*

ICONOCLASTIC CONTROVERSY

In the eighth and ninth centuries the question of the person and nature of Christ continued in the controversy over the veneration of the holy icons in the Church. At this time many were found, including emperors and secular rulers, who claimed that the veneration of icons is wrong because it is the sin of idolatry. They claimed that as God is invisible and has commanded in the Old Testament law that men are not to make "graven images," so it is wrong to depict and to honor images of Christ and the saints.

The defenders of the veneration of the holy icons, led by Saints John Damascene and Theodore Studion, claimed that the central point of the Christian faith is that **"the Word became flesh and dwelt among us"** and that **"we have beheld His glory"** (Jn 1.14). Referring to the holy scriptures they insisted that belief in the incarnation of the Son of God calls for the veneration of icons since Jesus Christ is a real man with a real human soul and body, and as such can be depicted. They said that those who were against the holy icons reduced the incarnation to a "fantasy" and denied the true humanity of the Son of God in His coming to man. Thus they made reference to the words of Jesus Himself in His dialogue with Philip:

> *Philip said to Him, "Lord, show us the Father and we shall be satisfied."*
>
> *Jesus said to him, "Have I been with you so long. and yet you do not know me, Philip? He who has seen me has seen the Father; how can you say, 'Show us the Father?'"* (Jn 14.8–9).

The defenders of the propriety of icon veneration also referred to the apostolic writings of Saint John and Saint Paul:

> *That which was from the beginning, which we have heard, which we have seen with our eyes, which we have looked upon and touched with our hands concerning the Word of Life the Life was made manifest, and we saw it . . .* (1 Jn 1.1–2).

... the god of this world has blinded the minds of the unbelievers to keep them from seeing the light of the gospel of the glory of Christ, who is the likeness [in Greek: eikōn] of God (2 Cor 4.4).

He is the image [eikōn] of the invisible God, the first born of all creation; for in Him all things were created, in heaven and on earth . . . all things were created through Him and for Him . . . for in Him all the fullness of God was pleased to dwell . . . (Colossians 1.15–20).

In many and various ways God spoke of old to our fathers by the prophets, but in these last days He has spoken to us by a Son, whom He appointed the heir of all things, through whom also He created the world. He is the reflection of the glory of God and the express image of His person, upholding the universe by the word of His power . . . (Hebrews 1.1–3).

The seventh ecumenical council in Nicea in 787 officially declared that the Christian faith is to be proclaimed "in words and images." And while making clear the teaching that holy icons may be made; that they are not to be worshipped—for only God Himself is worthy of worship—but are to be venerated and honored; the seventh council also made the following statement about Christ in reference to the veneration of icons:

... we keep unchanged all the ecclesiastical traditions handed down to us, whether in writing or verbally, one of which is the making of pictorial representations, agreeable to the history of the preaching of the Gospel, a tradition useful in many respects, but especially in this, that so the incarnation of the Word of God is shone forth in real and not merely in phantasy, for these have mutual indications and without doubt have also mutual significations.

In later times the doctrines of the real divinity and real humanity of Jesus Christ was witnessed and defended by such saints as Simeon the

New Theologian (d. 1022) and Gregory Palamas, the Archbishop of Thessalonika (d. 1359) in their teachings about the real sanctification and deification of man through living communion with God through Jesus Christ in the Holy Spirit in the Church. In and through Christ, the Word incarnate, human persons can be filled with the Spirit of God and can be in genuine communion with God the Father, participating in the uncreated being, life and light of the Most Blessed Trinity. If Jesus Christ were not true God and true Man, this would be impossible. But it is not impossible. It is man's experience of salvation and redemption in the life of the Church of Christ.

Redemption

> *And He was crucified for us under Pontius Pilate, and suffered, and was buried.*

Although Jesus did not sin and did not have to suffer and die, he voluntarily took upon himself the sins of the world and voluntarily gave himself up to suffering and death for the sake of salvation. This was his task as the Messiah-Saviour:

> *The Spirit of the Lord is upon me to bring good tidings to the afflicted . . . to bind up the broken-hearted, to proclaim liberty to the captives, and the opening of the prison to those who are bound . . . to comfort all who mourn . . . to give them a garland instead of ashes, the oil of gladness instead of mourning"* (Is 61.1–3).

And at the same time, Jesus had to do this as the **suffering servant of Yahweh-God.**

> *He was despised and rejected by men, a man of sorrows, and acquainted with grief, and as one from whom men hide their faces he was despised. and we esteemed him not.*

Surely he has borne our griefs and carried our sorrows, yet we esteemed him stricken, smitten by God and afflicted.

But he was wounded for our transgressions, he was bruised for our iniquities, upon him was the chastisement that made us whole, and by his stripes [i.e., wounds] we are healed.

All we like sheep have gone astray; we have turned everyone to his own way; and the Lord has laid on him the iniquity of us all.

He was oppressed, and he was afflicted, yet he opened not his mouth; like a lamb led to the slaughter, and like a sheep that before his shearers is dumb, so he opened not his mouth.

By oppression and judgement he was taken away . . . And they made his grave with the wicked, and with a rich man in his death, although he had done no violence, and there was no deceit in his mouth.

Yet it was the will of the Lord [Yahweh] to bruise him; he has put him to grief; when he makes himself an offering for sin, he shall see his offspring, he shall prolong his days; the will of the Lord shall prosper in his hand; he shall see the fruit of the travail of his soul and be satisfied; by his knowledge shall the righteous one, my servant, make many to be accounted righteous; and he shall bear their iniquities.

Therefore I will divide him a portion with the great and he shall divide the spoil with the strong; because he poured out his soul to death, and was numbered with the transgressors; yet he bore the sin of many [or the multitude] and made intercession for the transgressors.

(Is 53)

These words of the prophet Isaiah written centuries before the birth of Jesus tell the story of his Messianic mission. It began officially before the eyes of all in his baptism by John in the Jordan. By allowing himself to be baptized with the sinners though he had no sin, Jesus shows that he accepts his calling to be identified with the sinners: "the Beloved" of the Father and "the Lamb of God who takes away the sin of the world" (Jn 1.29; Mat 3.17).

Jesus begins to teach, and on the very day and at that very moment when his disciples first confess him to be the Messiah, "the Christ, the Son of the Living God," Jesus tells immediately of his mission to "go to Jerusalem and suffer many things . . . and be killed, and on the third day be raised" (Mt 16.16–23; Mk 8.29–33). The apostles are greatly upset by this. Jesus then immediately shows them his divinity by being transfigured before them in divine glory on the mountain in the presence of Moses and Elijah. He then tells them once more: "The Son of Man is to be delivered into the hands of men, and they will kill him, and he will be raised on the third day" (Mt 17.1–23; Mk 9.1–9).

The powers of evil multiplied against Christ at the end: "The kings of the earth counsel together against the Lord and His Christ" (Ps 2.2). They were looking for causes to kill him. The formal reason was blasphemy, "because you, being a man, make yourself God" (Jn 10.31–38). Yet the deep reasons were more personal: Jesus told men the truth and revealed their stubbornness, foolishness, hypocrisy, and sin. For this reason every sinner, hardened in his sins and refusing to repent, wishes and causes the crucifixion of Christ.

The death of Jesus came at the hands of the religious and political leaders of his time, with the approval of the masses: when Caiaphas was high priest, "under Pontius Pilate." He was "crucified for us . . . and suffered and was buried" in order to be with us in our sufferings and death which we brought upon ourselves because of our sins: "for the wages of sin are death" (Rom 6.23). In this sense the Apostle Paul writes of Jesus that "having become a curse for us" (Gal 3.13), "for our sake he (God the Father) made him to be sin who knew no sin, so that in him we might become the righteousness of God" (2 Cor 5.21).

The sufferings and death of Christ in obedience to the Father reveals the super-abundant divine love of God for his creation. For when all was sinful, cursed, and dead, Christ became sin, a curse, and dead for us—though he himself never ceased to be the righteousness and blessedness and life of God Himself. It is to this depth, of which lower and more base cannot be discovered or imagined, that Christ has humiliated himself "for us men and for our salvation." For being God, he became man; and being man, he became a slave; and being a slave, he became dead and not only dead, but dead on a cross. From this deepest degradation of God flows the eternal exaltation of man. This is the pivotal doctrine of the Orthodox Christian faith, expressed over and again in many ways throughout the history of the Orthodox Church. It is the doctrine of the *atonement*—for we are made to be "at one" with God. It is the doctrine of **redemption**—for we are redeemed, i.e., "bought with a price," the great price of the blood of God (Acts 20.28; 1 Cor 6.20).

> *Have this mind among yourselves which you have in Christ Jesus who, though He was in the form of God, did not count equality with God a thing to be grasped, but emptied Himself, taking the form of a servant [slave], being born in the likeness of men. And being found in human form, He humbled Himself and became obedient unto death, even death on a cross. Therefore God has highly exalted Him and bestowed on Him the name which is above every name, that at the name of Jesus every knee should bow, in heaven and on earth and under the earth, and every tongue confess that Jesus Christ is Lord, to the glory of God the Father* (Phil 2.5–11).

In contemplating the saving and redeeming action of Christ, it has become traditional to emphasize three aspects which in reality are not divided, and cannot be; but which in theory (i.e., in the **vision** of Christ's being.and activity as the Saviour of the world) may be distinguished. The first of these three aspects of the redeeming work of Christ is the fact that Jesus saves mankind by providing the perfect image and example of human life as filled with the grace and power of God.

JESUS, THE PERFECT IMAGE OF HUMAN LIFE

Christ is the incarnate Word of God. He is the Teacher and Master sent by God to the world. He is the embodiment of God Himself in human form. He is "the image of the invisible God" (Col 1.15). In Him "the fullness of divinity dwells bodily" (Col 2.9). The person who sees Jesus sees God the Father (Jn 14.9). He is the "reflection of the glory of God and the express image of His person" (Heb 1.3). He is the "light of the world" who "enlightens every man . . . coming into the world" (Jn 8.12, 1.9). To be saved by Jesus Christ is first of all to be enlightened by Him; to see Him as the Light, and to see all things in the light of Him. It is to know Him as "the Truth" (Jn 14.6); and to know the truth in Him.

> *And you will know the truth and the truth will make you free* (Jn 8.31).

When one is saved by God in Christ one comes to the knowledge of the truth, fulfilling God's desire for His creatures, for "God our Saviour . . . desires all men to be saved and to come to the knowledge of the truth" (1 Tim 2.4). In saving God's world, Jesus Christ enlightens God's creatures by the Holy Spirit, the Spirit of God who is the Spirit of Truth who proceeds from the Father and is sent into the world through Christ.

> *If you love Me, you will keep My commandments. And I will pray the Father, and He will give you another Counselor, to be with you forever, even the Spirit of Truth, whom the world cannot receive,*

because it neither sees Him nor knows Him; you know Him, for He dwells with you, and will be in you (Jn 14.15–17).

But the Counselor, the Holy Spirit, whom the Father will send in My name, He will teach you all things, and bring to your remembrance all that I have said to you . . . (Jn 15.26).

When the Spirit of Truth comes, He will guide you into all the truth . . . (Jn 16.13).

The first aspect of salvation in Christ, therefore, is to be enlightened by Him and to know the truth about God and man by the guidance of the Holy Spirit, the Spirit of Truth, which God gives through Him to those who believe. This is witnessed to in the apostolic writings of Saints John and Paul:

Now we have received not the spirit of the world, but the Spirit which is from God, that we might understand the gifts bestowed on us by God. And we impart this in words not taught by human wisdom, but taught by the Spirit, interpreting spiritual truths to those who possess the Spirit. . . . For who has known the mind of the Lord so as to instruct him? But we have the mind of Christ (1 Cor 2.13–16).

For [God] has made known to us in all wisdom and insight the mystery of His will, according to His purpose which He set forth in Christ as a plan for the fullness of time, to unite all things in Him, things in heaven and things on earth. . . . To me . . . this grace was given . . . to make all men see what is the plan of the mystery hidden for ages in God . . . that through the church the manifold wisdom of God might now be made known . . . (Eph 1.8–10; 3.9).

For I want . . . that their hearts may be encouraged as they are knit together in love, to have all the riches of assured understanding and the knowledge of God's mystery in Christ, in whom are hid all the treasures of wisdom and knowledge (Col 2.1–3).

But you have been anointed by the Holy One, and you know all things I write to you, not because you do not know the truth, but because you know it, and know that no lie is of the truth. . . . but the anointing which you received from Him abides in you, and you have no need that any one should teach you; as His anointing teaches you about everything, and is true and is no lie, just as it has taught you, abide in Him. . . . And by this we know that He abides in us, by the Spirit which He has given to us (1 Jn 2.20–27; 3.24).

The first aspect of man's salvation by God in Christ is, therefore, the ability and power to see, to know, to believe and to love the truth of God in Christ, who is the Truth, by the Spirit of Truth. It is the gift of knowledge and wisdom, of illumination and enlightenment, it is the condition of being "taught by God" as foretold by the prophets and fulfilled by Christ (Is 54.13; Jer 31.33–34; Jn 6.45). Thus, in the Orthodox Church, the entrance into the saving life of the Church through baptism and chrismation is called "holy illumination."

For it is God who said, "Let light shine out of darkness," who has shone in our hearts to give the light of the knowledge of the glory of God in the face of Christ (2 Cor 4.6).

JESUS, THE RECONCILER OF MAN WITH GOD

The second aspect of Christ's one, indivisible act of salvation of man and his world is the accomplishment of man's reconciliation with God the Father through the forgiveness of sins. This is the redemption and atonement strictly speaking, the release from sins, and the punishment due to sins; the being made "at one" with God.

While we were yet helpless, at the right time Christ died for the ungodly. Why, one will hardly die for a righteous man—though perhaps for a good man one will dare even to die. But God shows His love for us in that while we were yet sinners Christ died for us. Since therefore we are now made righteous by His blood, much more shall we be saved by Him from the wrath of God. For if while we were enemies we were reconciled to God by the death of His Son, much more, now that we are reconciled, shall we be saved by His life. Not only so, but we also rejoice in God through our Lord Jesus Christ, through whom we have now received our reconciliation (Rom 5.6–11).

Therefore if anyone is in Christ, he is a new creation; the old has passed away, behold, the new has come. All this is from God, who through Christ reconciled us to Himself and gave us the ministry of reconciliation; that is, God was in Christ reconciling the world to Himself, not counting their trespasses against them, and entrusting to us the message of reconciliation (2 Cor 5.17–19).

The forgiveness of sins is one of the signs of the coming of the Christ, the Messiah, as foretold in the Old Testament:

. . . they shall all know me, from the least to the greatest, says the Lord; for I will forgive their iniquity, and I will remember their sin no more (Jer 31.34).

Christ is the Lamb of God who takes away the sins of the world, the Lamb that is slain that through Him all sins might be forgiven. He is also the great high priest, who offers the perfect sacrifice by which man is purged from his sins and cleansed from his iniquities. Jesus offers, as high priest, the perfect sacrifice of His own very life, His own body, as the Lamb of God, upon the tree of the cross.

For to this you have been called, because Christ suffered for you, leaving you an example that you should follow in His steps. He committed no sin; no guile was found on His lips. When He was reviled, He did not revile in return; when He suffered, He did not threaten; but He trusted to Him who judges justly. He Himself bore our sins in His body on the tree, that we might die to sin and live to righteousness. By

His wounds you have been healed. For you were straying like sheep, but have now returned to the Pastor and Bishop of your souls (1 Pet 2.22–25).

The high-priestly offering and sacrifice of the Son of God to His eternal Father is described in great detail in the Letter to the Hebrews in the New Testament scriptures.

In the days of His flesh, Jesus offered up prayers and supplications, with loud cries and tears, to Him who was able to save Him from death, and He was heard for His godly fear. Although He was a Son, He learned obedience through what He suffered, and being made perfect, He became the source of eternal salvation to all who obey Him, being designated a high priest by God, according to the order of Melchizedek (Heb 5.7–10).

But when Christ appeared as a high priest of the good things that have come . . . He entered once for all into the Holy Place [not made by hands, i.e., the Presence of God] taking . . . His own blood, thus securing an eternal redemption. For if the sprinkling of defiled persons with the blood of goats and bulls and with the ashes of a heifer sanctifies for the purification of the flesh, how much more shall the blood of Christ who through the eternal Spirit offered Himself without blemish to God, purify your conscience from dead works to serve the living God. Therefore, He is the mediator of a new covenant, so that those who are called may receive the promised eternal inheritance, since a death has occurred which redeems them from the transgressions under the first covenant (Heb 9.11–15).

According to the scriptures, man's sins and the sins of the whole world are forgiven and pardoned by the sacrifice of Christ, by the offering of His life—His body and His blood, which is the "blood of God" (Acts 20.28)—upon the cross. This is the "redemption," the "ransom," the "expiation," the "propitiation" spoken about in the scriptures which had to be made so that man could be "at one" with God. Christ "paid the price" which was necessary to be paid for the world to be pardoned and cleansed of all iniquities and sins (1 Cor 6.20; 7.23).

In the history of Christian doctrine there has been great debate over the question of to whom Christ "pays the price" for the ransom of the world and the salvation of mankind. Some have said that the "payment" was made to the devil. This is the view that the devil received certain "rights" over man and his world because of man's sin. In his rebellion against God, man "sold himself to the devil" thus allowing the Evil One to become the "prince of this world" (Jn 12.31). Christ comes to pay the debt to the devil and to release man from his control by sacrificing Himself upon the cross.

Others say that Christ's "payment" on behalf of man had to be made to God the Father. This is the view which interprets Christ's sacrificial death on the cross as the proper punishment that had to be paid to satisfy God's wrath over the human race. God was insulted by man's sin. His law was broken and His righteousness was offended. Man had to pay the penalty for his sin by offering the proper punishment. But no amount of human punishment could satisfy God's justice because God's justice is divine. Thus the Son of God had to be born into the world and receive the punishment that was rightly to be placed on men. He had to die in order for God to receive proper satisfaction for man's offenses against Him. Christ substituted Himself on our behalf and died for our sins, offering His blood as the satisfying sacrifice for the sins of the world. By dying on the cross in place of sinful man, Christ pays the full and total payment for man's sins. God's wrath is removed. Man's insult is punished. The world is reconciled with its Creator.

Commenting on this question about to whom Christ "pays the price" for man's salvation, St Gregory the Theologian in the fourth century wrote the following in his second Easter Oration:

Now we are to examine another fact and dogma, neglected by most people, but in my judgment well worth enquiring into. To whom was that Blood offered that was shed for us, and why was It shed? I mean the precious and famous Blood of our God and High Priest and Sacrifice.

We were detained in bondage by the Evil One, sold under sin, and receiving pleasure in exchange for wickedness. Now, "since a ransom belongs only to him who holds in bondage, I ask to whom was this offered, and for what cause?

If to the Evil One, fie upon the outrage! If the robber receives ransom, not only from God, but a ransom which consists of God Himself, and has such an illustrious payment for his tyranny, then it would have been right for him to have left us alone altogether!

But if to God the Father, I ask first, how? For it was not by Him that we were being oppressed. And next, on what principle did the Blood of His only-begotten Son delight the Father, who would not receive even Isaac, when he was being sacrificed by his father, [Abraham], but changed the sacrifice by putting a ram in the place of the human victim? (see Gen 22).

Is it not evident that the Father accepts Him, but neither asked for Him nor demanded Him; but on account of the incarnation, and because Humanity must be sanctified by the Humanity of God, that He might deliver us Himself, and overcome the tyrant [i.e., the devil] and draw us to Himself by the mediation of His Son who also arranged this to the honor of the Father, whom it is manifest He obeys in all things.

In Orthodox theology generally it can be said that the language of "payment" and "ransom" is rather understood as a metaphorical and symbolical way of saying that Christ has done all things necessary to save and redeem mankind enslaved to the devil, sin and death, and under the wrath of God. He "paid the price," not in some legalistic or juridical or economic meaning. He "paid the price" not to the devil whose rights over man were won by deceit and tyranny. He "paid the price" not to God the Father in the sense that God delights in His sufferings and received "satisfaction" from His creatures in Him. He "paid the price" rather, we might say, to Reality Itself. He "paid the price" to create the conditions in and through which man might receive the forgiveness of sins and eternal life by dying and rising again in Him to newness of life (see Rom 5–8; Gal 2–4).

By dying on the cross and rising from the dead, Jesus Christ cleansed the world from evil and sin. He defeated the devil "in his own territory" and on "his own terms." The "wages of sin is death" (Rom 6.23). So the Son of God became man and took upon Himself the sins of the world and died a voluntary death. By His sinless and innocent death accomplished entirely by His free will — and not by physical, moral, or juridical necessity - He made death to die and to become itself the source and the way into life eternal. This is what the Church sings on the feast of the Resurrection, the New Passover in Christ, the new Paschal Lamb, who is risen from the dead:

> *Christ is risen from the dead!*
> *Trampling down death by death!*
> *And upon those in the tombs bestowing life!*
>
> (Easter Troparion)

And this is how the Church prays at the divine liturgy of Saint Basil the Great:

> *He was God before the ages, yet He appeared on earth and lived among men, becoming incarnate of a holy Virgin;*
> *He emptied Himself, taking the form of a servant, being likened to the body of our lowliness, that He might liken us to the image of His Glory.*

For as by man sin entered into the world, and death by sin, so it pleased Thine Only-begotten Son, who was in the bosom of Thee, the God and Father, who was born of a woman, the holy Theotokos and ever-virgin Mary, who was born under the law to condemn sin in His flesh, so that those who were dead in Adam might be made alive in Thy Christ Himself.

He lived in this world and gave commandments of salvation; releasing us from the delusions of idolatry, He brought us to knowledge of Thee, the true God and Father. He obtained us for His own chosen people, a royal priesthood, a holy nation.

Having cleansed us in water, and sanctified us with the Holy Spirit, He gave Himself as a ransom to death, in which we were held captive, sold under sin.

Descending through the cross into Sheol — that He might fill all things with Himself — He loosed the pangs of death. He arose on the third day, having made for all flesh a path to the resurrection from the dead, since it was not possible for the Author of Life to be a victim of corruption. So He became the first—fruits of those who have fallen asleep, the first-born of the dead, that He might be Himself truly the first in all things . . .

(Eucharistic Prayer of the Liturgy of St Basil)

JESUS, THE DESTROYER OF DEATH

The third and final aspect of the saving and redeeming action of Christ, therefore, is the deepest and most comprehensive. It is the destruction of death by Christ's own death. It is the transformation of death itself into an act of life. It is the recreation of Sheol—the spiritual condition of being dead—into the paradise of God. Thus, in and through the death of Jesus Christ, death is made to. die. In Him, who is the Resurrection and the Life, man cannot die, but lives forever with God.

Truly, truly I say to you, he who hears my word and believes in Him who sent me has eternal life; he does not come into judgment, but has passed from death into life (Jn 5.24).

I am the Resurrection and the Life! He who believes in me, though he die, yet shall he live, and whoever lives and believes in me shall never die (Jn 11.25–26).

It is Christ Jesus who died, yes, who was raised from the dead, who is at the right hand of God, who indeed intercedes for us! Who shall separate us from the love of Christ? . . . For I am sure that neither death, not life, nor angels, nor principalities, nor things present, nor things to come, not powers, nor height, nor depth, nor anything else in all creation will be able to separate us from the love of God in Christ Jesus our Lord (Rom 8.34–39).

For in Him the whole fullness of divinity dwells bodily, and you have come to fullness of life in Him . . . and you were buried with Him in baptism, in which you were also raised with Him through faith in the working of God who raised Him from the dead. And you were dead in trespasses . . . God made alive together with Him, having forgiven us all our trespasses, having cancelled the bond which stood against us with its legal demands; this He set aside, nailing it to the cross. He disarmed the [demonic] principalities and powers and made a public example of them, triumphing over them . . . for you have died, and your life is hid with Christ in God. (Colossians 2.9 ff.)

This is the doctrine of the New Testament scriptures, repeated over and again in many ways in the tradition of the Church: in its sacraments, hymnology, theology, iconography. Christ's victory over death is man's release from sins and man's victory over enslavement to the devil because in and through Christ's death man dies and is born again to eternal life. In his death sins are no longer counted. In his death the devil no longer holds him. In his death he is born again to newness of life and is liberated from all that is evil, false, demonic and sinful. In a word, he is freed from all that is dead by dying and rising again in and with Jesus.

> *But we see Jesus, who for a little while was made lower than the angels, crowned with glory and honor because of the suffering of death, so that by the grace of God He might taste death for every one. . . . Since therefore the children share in flesh and blood, He Himself likewise partook of the same nature, that through death He might destroy him who has the power of death, that is, the devil, and deliver all those who through fear of death were subject to lifelong bondage* (Heb 2.9–15).

> *But in fact Christ has been raised from the dead, the first-fruits of those who have fallen asleep. For as by a man came death, by a Man has come also the resurrection of the dead. For as in Adam all die, so also in Christ shall all be made alive. [. . .] The sting of death is sin, and the power of sin is the law. But thanks be to God who gives us the victory through our Lord Jesus Christ* (1 Cor 15.20 ff; 56–57).

Resurrection

> *And He rose again from the dead on the third day,*
> *according to the Scriptures . . .*

Christ is risen from the dead! This is the main proclamation of the Christian faith. It forms the heart of the Church's preaching, worship and spiritual life. ". . . if Christ has not been raised, then our preaching is in vain and your faith is in vain" (1 Cor 15.14).

In the first sermon ever preached in the history of the Christian Church, the Apostle Peter began his proclamation:

> *Men of Israel, hear these words; Jesus of Nazareth, a man attended to you by God with mighty works and signs and wonders which God did to him in your midst, as you yourself know—this Jesus delivered*

up according to a definite plan and foreknowledge of God, you cruci-
fied and killed by the hands of lawless men. But God raised him up,
having loosed the pains of death, because it was not possible for him
to be held by it (Acts 2.22–24).

Jesus had the power to lay down his life and the power to take it up again:

For this reason the Father loves me, because I lay down my life, that
I may take it again. No one takes it from me, but I lay it down of
my own accord. I have the power to lay it down, and I have the
power to take it again; this charge I have received from my father (Jn
10.17–18).

According to Orthodox doctrine there is no competition of "lives" between God and Jesus, and no competition of "powers." The power of God and the power of Jesus, the life of God and the life of Jesus, are one and the same power and life. To say that God has raised Christ, and that Christ has been raised by his own power is to say essentially the same thing. "For as the Father has life in himself," says Christ, so he has granted the Son also to have life in himself" (Jn 5.26). "I and the Father are one" (Jn 10.30).

The Scriptural stress that God has raised up Jesus only emphasizes once more that Christ has given his life, that he has laid it down fully, that he has offered it whole and without reservation to God—who then gave it back in his resurrection from the dead.

The Orthodox Church believes in Christ's real death and his actual resurrection. Resurrection, however, does not simply mean bodily resuscitation. Neither the Gospel nor the Church teaches that Jesus was lying dead and then was biologically revived and walked around in the same way that he did before he was killed. In a word, the Gospel does not say that the angel moved the stone from the tomb in order to let Jesus out. The angel moved the stone to reveal that Jesus was not there (Mk 16; Mt 28).

In his resurrection Jesus is in a new and glorious form. He appears in different places immediately. He is difficult to recognize (Lk 24.16; Jn 20.14). He eats and drinks to show that he is not a ghost (Lk 24.30, 39). He allows himself to be touched (Jn 20.27, 21.9). And yet he appears in the midst of disciples, "the doors being shut" (Jn 20.19, 26). And he "vanishes out of their sight" (Lk 24.31). Christ indeed is risen, but his resurrected humanity is full of life and divinity. It is humanity in the new form of the eternal life of the Kingdom of God.

> *So it is with the resurrection of the dead: What is sown is perishable, what is raised is imperishable. It is sown in dishonor, it is raked in glory. It is sown in weakness, it is raised in power. It is sown a physical body, it is raised a spiritual body.*
>
> *Thus, it is written, the first man Adam became a living being; the last Adam [i.e. Christ] became a life-giving spirit. But it is not the spiritual which is first but the physical, then the spiritual.*
>
> *The first man was from the earth, a man of dust; the second man is from heaven. As was the man of dust, so are those who are of the dust; and as is the man from heaven, so are those who are of heaven. Just as we have home the image of the man of dust, we shall also bear the image of the man of heaven (1 Cor 15.42–50).*

The resurrection of Christ is the first fruits of the resurrection of all humanity. It is the fulfillment of the Old Testament, "according to the Scriptures" where it is written, "For Thou doest not give me up unto Sheol [that is, the realm of death], or let Thy Godly one see corruption" (Ps 16.10; Acts 2.25–36). In Christ all expectations and hopes are filled: O Death, where is your sting? O Sheol, where is your victory? (Hos 13.14).

> *He will swallow up death forever, and the Lord God will wipe away tears from all faces . . . It will be said on that day, "Lo, this is our God; we have waited for Him; let us be glad and rejoice in His salvation"* (Is 25.8–9).

> *Come, let us return to the Lord: For He has torn, that He may heal us; He has stricken, and He will bind us up. After two days He will revive us; on the third day He will raise us up, that we may live before Him* (Hos 6.1–2).

> *Thus says the Lord God: Behold I will open your graves, and raise you from your graves, O my people . . . And you shall know that I am the Lord, when I open your graves, and raise you from your graves, O my people. And I will put my Spirit within you, and you shall live . . .* (Ezek 37.12–14).

On Death and Resurrection in Christ

Yesterday I was crucified with Him; today I am glorified with Him.

Yesterday I died with Him; today I am made alive with Him.

Yesterday I was buried with Him; today I am raised up with Him.

Let us offer to Him Who suffered and rose again for us . . .
ourselves, the possession most precious to God and most
proper.

Let us become like Christ, since Christ became like us.

Let us become Divine for His sake, since for us He became Man.

He assumed the worse that He might give us the better.

He became poor that by His poverty we might become rich.

He accepted the form of a servant that we might win back our
freedom.

He came down that we might be lifted up.

He was tempted that through Him we might conquer.

He was dishonored that He might glorify us.

He died that He might save us.

He ascended that He might draw to Himself us, who were thrown
down through the fall of sin.

Let us give all, offer all, to Him who gave Himself a Ransom and
Reconciliation for us.

We needed an incarnate God, a God put to death, that we might
live.

We were put to death together with Him that we might be
cleansed.

We rose again with Him because we were put to death with Him.

We were glorified with Him because we rose again with Him.

A few drops of Blood recreate the whole of creation!

—St Gregory the Theologian, *Easter Orations*

Ascension

and ascended into heaven, and sits at the right hand of the Father . . .

After his resurrection from the dead Jesus appeared to men for a period of forty days after which he "was taken up into heaven, and sat down

at the right hand of God" (Mk 16.19; see also Lk 24.50 and Acts 1.9–11).

The ascension of Jesus Christ is the final act of his earthly mission of salvation. The Son of God comes "down from heaven" to do the work which the Father gives him to do; and having accomplished all things, he returns to the Father bearing for all eternity the wounded and glorified humanity which he has assumed (see e.g. Jn 17).

The doctrinal meaning of the ascension is the glorification of human nature, the reunion of man with God. It is indeed, the very penetration of man into the inexhaustible depths of divinity.

We have seen already that "the heavens" is the symbolical expression in the Bible for the uncreated, immaterial, divine "realm of God" as one saint of the Church has called it. To say that Jesus is "exalted at the right hand of God" as St Peter preached in the first Christian sermon (Acts 2.33) means exactly this: that man has been restored to communion with God, to a union which is, according to Orthodox doctrine, far greater and more perfect than that given to man in his original creation (see Eph 1–2).

Man was created with the potential to be a "partaker of the divine nature," to refer to the Apostle Peter once more (2 Pet 1.4). It is this participation in divinity, called theosis (which literally means deification or divinization) in Orthodox theology, that the ascension of Christ has fulfilled for humanity. The symbolical expression of the "sitting at the right hand" of God means nothing other than this. It does not mean that somewhere in the created universe the physical Jesus is sitting in a material throne.

The *Letter to the Hebrews* speaks of Christ's ascension in terms of the Jerusalem Temple. Just as the high priests of Israel entered the "holy of holies" to offer sacrifice to God on behalf of themselves and the people, so Christ the one, eternal and perfect High Priest offers himself on the cross to God as the one eternal, and perfect, Sacrifice, not for himself but for all sinful men. As a man, Christ enters (once and for all) into the one eternal and perfect Holy of Holies: the very "Presence of God in the heavens."

> . . . *we have a great high priest who has passed through the heavens, Jesus, the Son of God . . .* (Heb 4.14)

> *For it was fitting that we should have such a high priest, holy, blameless, unstained, separated from sinners, exalted above the heavens. . . . He has no need like those high priests to offer sacrifice daily, first for his own sins and then for those of the people; he did this once and for all when he offered up himself.*
>
> *Now, the point in what we are saying is this: we have such a high priest, one who is seated at the right hand of the throne of the Majesty in heaven, a minister in the sanctuary and the true tabernacle which is set up not by man but by the Lord* (Heb 7.26; 8.2).

> *For Christ has entered, not into a sanctuary made with hands, a copy of the true one, but into heaven itself, now to appear in the presence of God on our behalf* (Heb 9.24).

. . . when Christ had offered for all time a single sacrifice for sins, he sat down at the right hand of God, then to wait until his enemies should be made a stool for his feet (Heb 10.12–13; Ps 110.1).

Thus, the ascension of Christ is seen as man's first entry into that divine glorification for which he was originally created. The entry is made possible by the exaltation of the divine Son who emptied himself in human flesh in perfect self-offering to God.

Judgment

and He will come again with glory to judge the living and the dead . . .

This Jesus who was taken up from you into heaven, will come the same way as you saw him go into heaven (Acts 1.11).

These words of the angels are addressed to the apostles at the ascension of the Lord. Christ will come again in glory, "not to deal with sin, but to save those who are eagerly waiting for him" (Heb 9.28).

For the Lord himself will descend from heaven with a cry of command, with the archangels' call, and with the sound of the trumpet of God. And the dead in Christ will rise first; then we who are alive, who are left, shall be caught up in the cloud to meet the Lord in the air, and so we shall always be with the Lord (1 Thess 4.16–17, the Epistle reading of the Orthodox funeral service).

The coming of the Lord at the end of the ages will be the Day of Judgment, the Day of the Lord foretold in the Old Testament and predicted by Jesus himself (e.g. Dan 7; Mt 24). The exact time of the end is not foretold, not even by Jesus, so that men would always be prepared by constant vigil and good works.

The very presence of Christ as the Truth and the Light is itself the judgment of the world. In this sense all men and the whole world are already judged or, more accurately, already live in the full presence of that reality—Christ and his works—by which they will be ultimately judged. With Christ now revealed, there is no longer any excuse for ignorance and sin (Jn 9.39).

At this point it is necessary to note that at the final judgment there will be those "on the left hand" who will go into "the eternal fire prepared for the devil and his angels" (Mt 25.41; Rev 20). That this is the case is no fault of God's. It is the fault only of men, for "as I hear, I judge and my judgment is just," says the Lord (Jn 5.30).

God takes no "pleasure in the death of the wicked" (Ezek 18.22). He "desires all men to be saved and to come to the knowledge of the Truth" (1 Tim 2.4). He does everything in His power so that salvation and eternal life would be available and possible for all. There is nothing more that God can do. Everything now depends on man. If some men refuse the gift of life in communion with God, the Lord can only honor this refusal and respect the freedom of His creatures which He Himself has given and will not take back. God allows men to live "with the devil and his angels" if they so desire. Even in this He is loving and just. For if God's presence as the "consuming fire" (Heb 12.29) and the "unapproachable light" (1 Tim 6.16) which delights those who love Him only produces hatred and anguish in those who do not "love His appearing" (2 Tim 4.8), there is nothing that God can do except either to destroy His sinful creatures completely, or to destroy Himself. But God will exist and will allow His creatures to exist. He also will not hide His Face forever.

The doctrine of eternal hell, therefore, does not mean that God actively tortures people by some unloving and perverse means. It does not mean that God takes delight in the punishment and pain of His people whom He loves. Neither does it mean that God "separates Himself" from His people, thus causing them anguish in this separation (for indeed if people hate God, separation would be welcome, and not abhorred!). It means rather that God continues to allow all people, saints and sinners alike, to exist forever. All are raised from the dead into everlasting life: "those who have done good, to the resurrection of judgment" (Jn 5.29). In the end, God will be "all and in all" (1 Cor 15.28). For those who love God, resurrection from the dead and the presence of God will be paradise. For those who hate God, resurrection from the dead and the presence of God will be hell. This is the teaching of the fathers of the Church.

There is sprung up a light for the righteous, and its partner is joyful gladness. And the light of the righteous is everlasting . . .

One light alone let us shun—that which is the offspring of the sorrowful fire . . .

For I know a cleansing fire which Christ came to send upon the earth, and He Himself is called a Fire. This Fire takes away whatsoever is material and of evil quality; and this He desires to kindle with all speed . . .

I know also a fire which is not cleansing, but avenging . . . which He pours down on all sinners . . . that which is prepared for the devil and his angels . . . that which proceeds from the Face of the Lord and shall burn up His enemies round about . . . the unquenchable fire which . . . is eternal for the wicked. For all these belong to the destroying power, though some may prefer even in this place to take a more merciful view of this fire, worthily of Him who chastises.

(St Gregory the Theologian)

. . . those who find themselves in Gehenna will be chastised with the scourge of love. How cruel and bitter this torment of love will be! For those who understand that they have sinned against love undergo greater sufferings than those produced of the most fearful tortures. The sorrow which takes hold of the heart which has sinned against love is more piercing than any other pain. It is not right to say that sinners in hell are deprived of the love of God . . . But love acts in two different ways, as suffering in the reproved, and as joy in the blessed.

(St Isaac of Syria)

Thus, man's final judgment and eternal destiny depends solely on whether or not man loves God and his brethren. It depends on whether or not man loves the light more than the darkness—or the darkness more than the light. It depends, we might say, on whether or not man loves Love and Light Itself; whether or not man loves Life—which is God Himself; the God revealed in creation, in all things, in the "least of the brethren."

The conditions of the final judgment are already known. Christ has given them Himself with absolute clarity.

> *When the Son of Man shall come in His glory, and all the angels with Him, then He will sit on His glorious throne. Before Him will be gathered all the nations and He will separate them one from another as a shepherd separates the sheep from the goats, and He will place the sheep at His right hand, but the goats at the left. Then the King will say to those at His right hand, "Come, O blessed of my Father, inherit the kingdom prepared for you from the foundation of the world; for I was hungry and you gave me food, I was thirsty and you gave me drink, I was a stranger and you welcomed me, I was naked and you clothed me, I was sick and you visited me, I was in prison and you came to me."*
>
> *Then the righteous will answer Him, "Lord, when did we see Thee hungry and feed Thee, or thirsty and give Thee drink? And when did we see Thee a stranger and welcome Thee, or naked and clothe Thee? And when did we see Thee sick or in prison and visit Thee?"*
>
> *And the King will answer them, "Truly, I say to you, as you did it to one of the least of these my brethren, you did it to me."*
>
> *Then He will say to those at His left hand, "Depart from me, you cursed, into the eternal fire prepared for the devil and his angels; for I was hungry and you gave me no food, I was thirsty and you gave me no drink, I was a stranger and you did not welcome me, naked and you did not clothe me, sick and in prison and you did not visit me."*

Then they also will answer, "Lord, when did we see Thee hungry
or thirsty or a stranger or naked or sick or in prison, and did not
minister to Thee?"

Then He will answer them, "Truly, I say to you, as you did it not
to one of the least of these, you did it not to me." And they will go away
into eternal punishment, but the righteous into eternal life.

(Mt 25.31–46, Gospel reading for Meatfare Sunday)

It is Christ who will judge, not God the Father. Christ has received
the power of judgment "because He is the Son of Man" (Jn 5.27).
Thus, man and the world are not judged by God "sitting on a cloud,"
as it were, but by One who is truly a man, the One who has suffered
every temptation of this world and has emerged victorious. The world
is judged by Him who was Himself hungry, thirsty, a stranger, naked,
in prison, wounded, and yet the salvation of all. As the Crucified One,
Christ has justly achieved the authority to make judgment for He
alone has been the perfectly obedient servant of the Father who knows
the depths of human tragedy by His own experience.

For He will render to every man according to his works: to those who
by patience in well-doing seek for glory and honor and immortality,
He will give eternal life; but for those who are factious and do not obey
the truth, but obey wickedness, there will be wrath and fury. There
will be tribulation and distress for every human being who does evil
. . . but glory and honor and peace for every one who does good . . .
for God shows no partiality. All who have sinned without the law, and
all who have sinned under the law will be judged by the law. For it is
not the hearers of the law who are righteous before God, but the doers
of the law who will be justified (Rom 2.6ff).

Kingdom of God

And of his kingdom there will be no end . . .

Jesus is the royal Son of David, of whom it was prophesied by the angel at his birth:

> *He will be great, and will be called the Son of the Most High; and the Lord will give to him the throne of his father David, and he will reign over the house of Jacob forever; and of his kingdom there will be no end* (Lk 1.32–33).

Through his sufferings as the Christ, Jesus achieved everlasting kingship and lordship over all creation. He has become "King of kings and Lord of lords," sharing this title with God the Father Himself (Deut 10.17; Dan 2.47; Rev 19.16). As a man, Jesus Christ is King of the Kingdom of God.

Christ came for no other reason than to bring God's kingdom to men. His very first public words are exactly those of his forerunner, John the Baptist: "Repent for the kingdom of heaven is at hand" (Mt 3.2, 4.17).

All through his life Jesus spoke of the kingdom. In the sermons such as the Sermon on the Mount and the many parables, he told of the everlasting kingdom.

> *Blessed are the poor in spirit for theirs is the kingdom of heaven . . .*
>
> *Blessed are they who are persecuted for righteousness sake for theirs is the kingdom of heaven.*
>
> *He who does these commandments and teaches them shall be called great in the kingdom of heaven.*
>
> *But seek ye first the kingdom of heaven and its righteousness, and all things will be yours as well.*

Not everyone who says to me, "Lord, Lord," shall enter the king-
dom of heaven, but he who does the will of my Father who is in
heaven.

(Mt 5–7)

The mustard seed, the leaven, the pearl of great price, the lost coin, the treasure in the field, the fishing net, the wedding feast, the banquet, the house of the Father, the vineyard . . . all are signs of the kingdom which Jesus has come to bring. And on the night of His last supper with the disciples He tells the apostles openly:

You are those who have continued with me in my trials; as my Father
appointed a kingdom for me, so do I appoint for you that you may
eat and drink at my table in my kingdom, and sit on thrones judging
the twelve tribes of Israel (Lk 22: 28–30; Reading of the Vigil of
Holy Thursday).

Christ's kingdom is "not of this world" (Jn 18.31). He says this to Pontius Pilate when being mocked as king, revealing in this humiliation His genuine divine kingship. The Kingdom of God, which Christ will rule, will come with power at the end of time when the Lord will fill all creation and will be truly "all, and in all" (Col 3.11). The Church, which in popular Orthodox doctrine is called the Kingdom of God on earth, has already mysteriously been given this experience. In the Church, Christ is already acknowledged, glorified, and served, as the only king and lord; and His Holy Spirit, whom the saints of the Church have identified with the Kingdom of God, is already given to the world in the Church with full graciousness and power.

The Kingdom of God, therefore, is a Divine Reality. It is the reality of God's presence among men through Christ and the Holy Spirit. "For the Kingdom of God . . . means . . . peace and joy and righteousness in the Holy Spirit" (Rom 14.17). The Kingdom of God as a spiritual, divine reality is given to men by Christ in the Church. It is celebrated and participated in the sacramental mysteries of the faith. It is witnessed to in the scriptures, the councils, the canons, and the saints. It will become the universal, final cosmic reality for the whole of creation at the end of the ages when Christ comes in glory to fill all things with Himself by the Holy Spirit, that God might be "all and in all" (1 Cor 15.28).

Holy Spirit

And in the Holy Spirit, Lord and Giver of Life, who proceeds from the Father, who together with the Father and the Son is worshipped and glorified, who spoke by the prophets . . .

The Holy Spirit bears the title of Lord with God the Father and Christ the Son. He is the Spirit of God and Spirit of Christ. He is eternal, uncreated, and divine; always existing with the Father and the Son; perpetually worshipped and glorified with them in the oneness of the Holy Trinity.

Just like the Son, there was no time when there was no Holy Spirit. The Spirit is before creation. He comes forth from God, as does the Son, in a timeless, eternal **procession**. "He proceeds from the Father," in eternity in a divinely instantaneous and perpetual movement (Jn 15.26).

Orthodox doctrine confesses that God the Father is the eternal origin and source of the Spirit, just as He is the source of the Son. Yet, the Church affirms as well that the manner of the Father's possession and production of the Spirit and the Son differ according to the difference between the Son being "born," and the Spirit "proceeding." There have been many attempts—by holy men inspired by God and with a genuine experience of His Trinitarian life to explain the distinction between the procession of the Spirit and the begetting or generation of the Son. For us it is enough to see that the difference between the two lies in the distinction between the divine persons and actions of the Son and the Spirit in relation to the Father, and so as well to each other and to the world. It is necessary to note further that all words and concepts about God and divinity, including those of "procession" and "generation" must give way before the mystical vision of the actual Divine Reality which they express. God may somehow be grasped by men as He has chosen to reveal Himself. However, the essence of His Triune existence remains—and will always remain—essentially inconceivable and inexpressible to created minds and lips. This does not mean that words about God are meaningless. It only means that they are inadequate to the Reality which they seek to express . . .

At this point also it is necessary to note that the Roman and Protestant churches differ in their credal statement about God by adding that the Holy Spirit proceeds from the Father "and the Son" (*filioque*)—a doctrinal addition unacceptable to Orthodoxy since it is both unscriptural and inconsistent with the Orthodox vision of God.

With the affirmation of the divinity of the Holy Spirit, and the necessity of worshipping and glorifying him with the Father and the Son, the Orthodox Church affirms that the Divine Reality, called also the **Deity** or the **Godhead** in the Orthodox Tradition, is the Holy Trinity.

The Holy Spirit is essentially one in his eternal existence with the Father and the Son; and so, in every action of God toward the world, the Holy Spirit is necessarily acting. Thus, in the Genesis account of creation it is written: "The Spirit of God was moving over the face of the waters" (Gen 1.2). It is this same Spirit who is the "breath of life" for all living things and particularly for man, made in the image and likeness of God (Gen 1.30; 2.7). Generally speaking the Spirit in Hebrew is called the "breath" or the "wind" of Yahweh. It is he who makes everything alive, the "giver of life" who upholds and sustains the universe in its existence and life (e.g. Ps 104.29; Job 33.4).

The Holy Spirit is also he who inspires the saints to speak God's word and to do God's will. He anoints the prophets, priests, and kings of the Old Testament; and "in the fullness of time" it is this same Spirit who "descends and remains" on Jesus of Nazareth, making him the Messiah (anointed) of God and manifesting him as such to the world. Thus, in the New Testament at the first **epiphany** (which means literally showing forth or manifestation) of Christ as the Messiah—his baptism by John in the Jordan—the Holy Spirit is revealed as descending and resting upon him "as a dove from heaven" (Jn 1.32; Lk 3.22, see also Mt 3.16 and Mk 1.9). It is important to note, both here and in the account of the Spirit's coming on the Day of Pentecost, as well as in other places in the Scriptures, that the words "as" and "like" are used in order to avoid an incorrect "physical" interpretation of the events recorded where the Bible itself is literally speaking in quite a symbolical and metaphorical way.

Jesus begins his public work after his baptism, and immediately refers Isaiah's prophecy about the Messiah directly to himself: "The Spirit of the Lord is upon me . . ." (Is 61.1; Lk 4.18).

All the days of his life Jesus is "full of the Holy Spirit"—preaching, teaching, healing, casting out devils and accomplishing every sign and wonder of his messiahship by the Spirit's power (Lk 4.11). It is written that even his self-offering to God on the cross is made "through the eternal Spirit" (Heb 9.14). And it is through the same divine Spirit that he and all men with him are risen from the dead (Ezek 37.1–4).

On the day of Pentecost the Holy Spirit comes upon the disciples of Christ in the form of "tongues as of fire," with the sound "like that of a mighty rushing wind" (Acts 2.1–4). We note once more the use of "as" and "like." The coming of the Spirit on Pentecost is the final fulfillment of Christ's earthly messianic mission, the beginning of the Christian Church. It is the fulfillment of the Old Testamental prophecy that in the time of the messiah-king, the Spirit of God will be "poured out on all flesh" (Joel 2.28; Acts 1.14). It is the condition of the age of the final and everlasting covenant of perfect mercy and peace (Ezek 34.37; Jer 31–33; Is 11.42, 44, 61).

The Christian Church lives by the Holy Spirit. The Spirit alone is the guarantee of God's Kingdom on earth. He is the sole guarantee that God's life and truth and love are with men. Only by the Holy Spirit can man and the world fulfill that for which they were created by God. All of God's actions toward man and the world—in creation, salvation and final glorification—are from the Father through the Son (Word) in the Holy Spirit; and all of man's capabilities of response to God are in the same Spirit, through the same Son to the same Father.

The Holy Spirit is the Spirit of life.

If the Spirit of him who raised Jesus from the dead dwells in you, he who raised Jesus from the dead will give life to your mortal bodies through the Spirit who dwells in you (Rom 8.11).

The Holy Spirit is the Spirit of truth.

When the Spirit of Truth comes he will guide you into all the Truth; for he will not speak on his own authority, but whatever he hears he will speak, and he will declare to you the things that are to come (Jn 16.13; see also Jn 14.25; Jn 15.26).

The Holy Spirit is the Spirit of divine sonship.

For all who are led by the Spirit are sons of God. For you did not receive the Spirit of slavery. . . . but you received the Spirit of sonship. When we cry "Abba! Father!" it is the Spirit himself bearing witness with our spirit that we are children of God (Rom 8.14; also Gal 4.6).

The Holy Spirit is the personal presence of the new and everlasting covenant between God and man, the seal and guarantee of the Kingdom of God, the power of the divine indwelling of God in man.

> *. . . you are a letter from Christ, delivered by us, written not with ink but with the Spirit of the living God, not on tablets of stone but on tablets of human hearts. . . . our sufficiency is from God who has qualified us to be ministers of a new covenant, not in written code but in the Spirit, for the written code kills, but the Spirit gives life* (2 Cor 3.2–6).

> *Do you not know that you are God's temple and that God's Spirit dwells in you . . . For God's temple is holy, and that temple you are* (1 Cor 3.16; also Rom 6.19).

> *. . . through him [Christ] we both have access in one Spirit to the Father. So then you are no longer strangers and sojourners but you are fellow citizens with the saints and members of the household of God, built upon the foundation of apostles and the prophets, Christ Jesus himself being the cornerstone, in whom the whole structure is joined together and grows in a holy temple in the Lord; in whom you also are built into it for a dwelling place of God in the Spirit* (Eph 2.18–22; also 1 Pet 2.4–9).

In the Holy Spirit men have the possibility of receiving every gift from God, of sharing His divine nature and life, of doing what Christ has done by fulfilling his "new commandment" to love one another even as he has loved us, "because God's love has been poured into our hearts through the Holy Spirit which he has given us" (Rom 5.5).

The fruit of the Spirit is love, joy, peace, patience, kindness, goodness, faithfulness, gentleness, self-control . . . . And those who belong to Christ Jesus have crucified the flesh with its passions and desires. If we live by the Spirit . . . he who sows to the Spirit will from the Spirit reap eternal life (Gal 5.22–25; 6.8).

Church

In one, holy, catholic and apostolic Church . . .

Church as a word means those called as a particular people to perform a particular task. The Christian Church is the assembly of God's chosen people called to keep his word and to do his will and his work in the world and in the heavenly kingdom.

In the Scriptures the Church is called the Body of Christ (Rom 12; 1 Cor 10, 12; Col 1) and the Bride of Christ (Eph 5; Rev 21). It is likened as well to God's living Temple (Eph 2; 1 Pet 2) and is called "the pillar and bulwark of Truth" (1 Tim 3.15).

ONE CHURCH

The Church is one because God is one, and because Christ and the Holy Spirit are one. There can only be one Church and not many. And this one Church, because its unity depends on God, Christ, and the Spirit, may never be broken. Thus, according to Orthodox doctrine, the Church is indivisible; men may be in it or out of it, but they may not divide it.

According to Orthodox teaching, the unity of the Church is man's free unity in the truth and love of God. Such unity is not brought about or established by any human authority or juridical power, but by God alone. To the extent that men are in the truth and love of God, they are members of His Church.

Orthodox Christians believe that in the historical Orthodox Church there exists the full possibility of participating totally in the Church of God, and that only sins and false human choices (heresies) put men outside of this unity. In non-Orthodox Christian groups the Orthodox claim that there are certain formal obstacles, varying in different groups, which, if accepted and followed by men, will prevent their perfect unity with God and will thus destroy the genuine unity of the Church (e.g., the papacy in the Roman Church).

Within the unity of the Church man is what he is created to be and can grow for eternity in divine life in communion with God through Christ in the Holy Spirit. The unity of the Church is not broken by time or space and is not limited merely to those alive upon the earth. The unity of the Church is the unity of the Blessed Trinity and of all of those who live with God: the holy angels, the righteous dead, and those who live upon the earth according to the commandments of Christ and the power of the Holy Spirit.

HOLY CHURCH

The Church is holy because God is holy, and because Christ and the Holy Spirit are holy. The holiness of the Church comes from God. The members of the Church are holy to the extent that they live in communion with God.

Within the earthly Church, people participate in God's holiness. Sin and error separate them from this divine holiness as it does from the divine unity. Thus, the earthly members and institutions of the Church cannot be identified as such with the Church as holy.

The faith and life of the Church on earth is expressed in its doctrines, sacraments, scriptures, services, and saints which maintain the Church's essential unity, and which can certainly be affirmed as "holy" because of God's presence and action in them.

CATHOLIC CHURCH

The Church is also catholic because of its relation to God, Christ, and the Holy Spirit. The word catholic means full, complete, whole, with nothing lacking. God alone is full and total reality; in God alone is there nothing lacking.

Sometimes the catholicity of the Church is understood in terms of the Church's universality throughout time and space. While it is true that the Church is universal—for all men at all times and in all places—this universality is not the real meaning of the term "catholic" when it is used to define the Church. The term "catholic" as originally used to define the Church (as early as the first decades of the second century) was a definition of quality rather than quantity. Calling the Church catholic means to define how it is, namely, full and complete, all-embracing, and with nothing lacking.

Even before the Church was spread over the world, it was defined as catholic. The original Jerusalem Church of the apostles, or the early city-churches of Antioch, Ephesus, Corinth, or Rome, were catholic. These churches were catholic—as is each and every Orthodox church today—because nothing essential was lacking for them to be the genuine Church of Christ. God Himself is fully revealed and present in each church through Christ and the Holy Spirit, acting in the local community of believers with its apostolic doctrine, ministry (hierarchy), and sacraments, thus requiring nothing to be added to it in order for it to participate fully in the Kingdom of God.

To believe in the Church as catholic, therefore, is to express the conviction that the fullness of God is present in the Church and that nothing of the "abundant life" that Christ gives to the world in the Spirit is lacking to it (Jn 10.10). It is to confess exactly that the Church is indeed "the fullness of him who fills all in all" (Eph 1.23; also Col 2.10).

APOSTOLIC CHURCH

The word apostolic describes that which has a mission, that which has "been sent" to accomplish a task.

Christ and the Holy Spirit are both "apostolic" because both have been sent by the Father to the World. It is not only repeated in the Scripture on numerous occasions how Christ has been sent by the Father, and the Spirit sent through Christ from the Father, but it also has been recorded explicitly that Christ is "the apostle . . . of our confession" (Heb 3.1).

As Christ was sent from God, so Christ Himself chose and sent His apostles. "As the Father has sent me, even so I send you . . . receive ye the Holy Spirit," the risen Christ says to His disciples. Thus, the apostles go out to the world, becoming the first foundation of the Christian Church.

In this sense, then, the Church is called apostolic: first, as it is built upon Christ and the Holy Spirit sent from God and upon those apostles who were sent by Christ, filled with the Holy Spirit; and secondly, as the Church in its earthly members is itself sent by God to bear witness to His Kingdom, to keep His word and to do His will and His works in this world.

Orthodox Christians believe in the Church as they believe in God and Christ and the Holy Spirit. Faith in the Church is part of the creedal statement of Christian believers. The Church is herself an object of faith as the divine reality of the Kingdom of God given to men by Christ and the Holy Spirit; the divine community founded by Christ against which "the gates of hell shall not prevail" (Mt 16.18).

The Church, and faith in the Church, is an essential element of Christian doctrine and life. Without the Church as a divine, mystical, sacramental, and spiritual reality, in the midst of the fallen and sinful world there can be no full and perfect communion with God. The Church is God's gift to the world. It is the gift of salvation, of knowledge and enlightenment, of the forgiveness of sins, of the victory over darkness and death. It is the gift of communion with God through Christ and the Holy Spirit. This gift is given totally, once and for all, with no reservations on God's part. It remains forever, until the close of the ages: invincible and indestructible. Men may sin and fight against the Church, believers may fall away and be separated from the Church, but the Church itself, the "pillar and bulwark of the truth" (1 Tim 3.15) remains forever.

> . . . *[God] has put all things under His [Christ's] feet and has made Him the head over all things for the Church, which is His body, the fullness of Him who fills all in all.*
>
> *. . . for through Him we . . . have access in one Spirit, to the Father. So then you are no longer strangers and sojourners, but you are fellow-citizens with the saints and members of the household of God, built upon the foundation of the apostles and prophets, Christ Jesus Himself being the cornerstone, in whom the whole structure is joined together and grows into a holy temple in the Lord; in whom you also are built into it for a dwelling place of God in the Spirit.*
>
> *. . . Christ loved the Church and gave Himself up for her, that he might sanctify her by the washing of water with the word, that He might present the Church to Himself in splendor, without spot or wrinkle or any such thing, that she might be holy and without blemish . . . This is a Great Mystery . . . Christ and the Church . . .*
>
> (Eph 1.21–23; 2.19–22; 5.25–32)

Sacraments

I confess one baptism for the remission of sins

The way of entry into the Christian Church is by baptism in the name of the Father and of the Son and of the Holy Spirit (Mt 28.19; the Baptismal Gospel reading in the Orthodox Church).

Baptism as a word means immersion or submersion in water. It was practiced in the Old Testament and even in some pagan religions as the sign of death and re-birth. Thus, John the Baptist was baptizing as the sign of new life and repentance which means literally a change of mind, and so of desires and actions in preparation of the coming of the Kingdom of God in Christ.

In the Church, the meaning of baptism is death and rebirth in Christ. It is the personal experience of Easter given to each man, the real possibility to die and to be "born anew" (Jn 3.3).

Do you not know that all of us who have been baptized into Christ Jesus were baptized into his death? We were buried therefore with him by baptism into death, so that as Christ was raised from the dead by the glory of the Father, we too might walk in newness of life. For if we have been united with him in a death like his, we shall certainly be united with him in a resurrection like his (Rom 6.3–5; Baptismal Epistle reading in the Orthodox Church; See also Col 2.12; 3.1).

The baptismal experience is the fundamental Christian experience, the primary condition for the whole of Christian life. Everything in the Church has its origin and context in baptism for everything in the Church originates and lives by the resurrection of Christ. Thus, following baptism comes "the seal of the gift of the Holy Spirit," the mystery (sacrament) of chrismation which is man's personal experience of Pentecost. And the completion and fulfillment of these fundamental Christian mysteries comes in the mystery of Holy Communion with God in the divine liturgy of the Church.

Only persons who are committed to Christ in the Orthodox Church through baptism and chrismation may offer and receive the holy eucharist in the Orthodox Church. The holy eucharist is Holy Communion. As such it is not just a "means of sanctification" for individual believers, a means through which private persons gain "communion" with God according to their own private consciences, beliefs and practices. It is rather the all-embracing act of Holy Communion of many persons having the same faith, the same hope, the same baptism. It is the corporate act of many persons having one mind, one heart, one mouth in the service of the one God and Lord, in the one Christ and the one Holy Spirit.

To participate in Holy Communion in the Orthodox Church is to identify oneself fully with all of the members of the Orthodox faith, living and dead; and to identify oneself fully with every aspect of the Orthodox Church: its history, councils, canons, dogmas, disciplines. It is to "take on oneself" the direct and concrete responsibility for everyone and everything connected in and with the Orthodox tradition and to profess responsibility for the everyday life of the Orthodox Church. It is to say before God and men that one is willing to be judged, in time and eternity, for what the Orthodox Church is and for what the Orthodox Church stands for in the midst of the earth.

Entering into the "Holy Communion" of the Orthodox Church through baptism and chrismation, one lives according to the life of the Church in every possible way. One is first of all faithful to the doctrine and discipline of the Church by faithful communion with the hierarchy of the Church who are those members of the Body sacramentally responsible for the teachings and practices of the Church; the sacramental images of the Church's identity and continuity in all places and all times. When one enters into the community of marriage, a union of one man and one woman forever according to the teaching of Jesus Christ, this union is sanctified and made eternal and divine in the sacramental mystery of matrimony in the Church. When one is sick and suffering, he "calls for the priests of the Church" to "pray over him, anointing him with oil" in the sacramental mystery of holy unction (cf. Jas 5.4). When one sins and falls away from the life of the Church, one returns to the "Holy Communion" of the divine community by the sacramental mystery of confession and repentance.

And when one dies, he is returned to his Creator in the midst of the Church, with the prayers and intercessions of the faithful brothers and sisters in Christ and the Spirit. Thus the entire life of the person is lived in and with the Church as the life of fullness and newness in God Himself, the Church which is the mystical presence of God's Kingdom which is not of this world.

The confession of "one baptism for the remission of sins," therefore, is the confession of the total newness of life given to men in the Church because Christ is risen.

> *If then you have been raised with Christ, seek the things that are above, where Christ is, seated at the right hand of God. Set your minds on things that are above, not on things that are on earth. For you have died and your life is hid with Christ in God. When Christ who is our life appears, then you also will appear with Him in glory* (Col 3.1–4).

Thus, in the Church, the whole of life is the one which begins in the new birth of baptism, the "life hid with Christ in God." All of the mysteries of the Christian faith are contained in this new life. Everything in the Church flows out of the waters of baptism: the remission of sins and life eternal.

Eternal Life

I look for the resurrection of the dead and the life of the world [ages] to come.

The Orthodox Church does not believe merely in the immortality of the soul, and in the goodness and ultimate salvation of only spiritual reality. Following the Scriptures, Orthodox Christians believe in the goodness of the human body and of all material and physical creation. Thus, in its faith in resurrection and eternal life, the Orthodox Church looks not to some "other world" for salvation, but to this very world so loved by God, resurrected and glorified by Him, tilled with His own divine presence.

At the end of the ages God will reveal His presence and will fill all creation with Himself. For those who love Him it will be paradise. For those who hate Him it will be hell. And all physical creation, together with the righteous, will rejoice and be glad in His coming.

> *The wilderness and the solitary places will be glad; the desert shall rejoice and blossom in abundance* (Is 35.1).

> *For behold I create new heavens and a new earth says the Lord, and the former things shall not be remembered or come to mind. But be glad and rejoice forever in that which I create, for behold I create Jerusalem a rejoicing and her people a joy* (Is 65.17–18).

The visions of the prophets and those of the Christian apostles about things to come are one and the same:

> *Then I saw a new heaven and a new earth: for the first heaven and the first earth had passed away, and the sea was no more. And I saw the holy city, new Jerusalem, coming down out of heaven from God, prepared as a bride adorned for her husband; and I heard a great voice from the throne saying, "Behold, the dwelling of God is with men. He will dwell with them, and they shall be His people, and God himself will be with them; He will wipe away every tear from their eyes, and death shall be no more, neither shall there be mourning nor crying nor pain any more, for the former things have passed away"* (Rev 21.1–5).

When the Kingdom of God fills all creation, all things will be made new. This world will again be that paradise for which it was originally created. This is the Orthodox doctrine of the final fate of man and his universe.

It is sometimes argued, however, that this world will be totally destroyed and that God will create everything new "out of nothing" by the act of a second creation. Those who hold this opinion appeal to such texts as that found in the second letter of Saint Peter:

> *But the day of the Lord will come like a thief, and then the heavens will pass away . . . and the elements will be dissolved with fire, and the earth and the works that are upon it will be burned up* (2 Pet 3.10).

Because the Bible never speaks about a "second creation" and because it continually and consistently witnesses that God loves the world which He has made and does everything that He can to save it, the Orthodox Tradition never interprets such scriptural texts as teaching the actual annihilation of creation by God. It understands such texts as speaking metaphorically of the great catastrophe which creation must endure, including even the righteous, in order for it to be cleansed, purified, made perfect, and saved. It teaches as well that there is an "eternal fire" for the ungodly, an eternal condition of their being destroyed. But in any case the "trial by fire" which "destroys the ungodly" is in no way understood by the Orthodox in the sense that creation is doomed to total destruction, despised by the loving Lord who created it and called it "very good" (Gen 1.31; also 1 Cor 3.13–15; Heb 12.25–29; Is 66; Rev 20–22).

the HOLY TRINITY

The Doctrine of the Holy Trinity

The doctrine of the Holy Trinity is not merely an "article of faith" which men are called to "believe." It is not simply a dogma which the Church requires its good members to "accept on faith." Neither is the doctrine of the Holy Trinity the invention of scholars and academicians, the result of intellectual speculation and philosophical thinking.

The doctrine of the Holy Trinity arises from man's deepest experiences with God. It comes from the genuine living knowledge of those who have come to know God in faith.

The paragraphs which follow are intended to show something of what God has revealed of Himself to the saints of the Church. To grasp the words and concepts of the doctrine of the Trinity is one thing; to know the Living Reality of God behind these words and concepts is something else. We must work and pray so that we might pass beyond every word and concept about God and to come to know Him for ourselves in our own living union with Him: "The Father through the Son in the Holy Spirit" (Eph 2: 18–22).

The Holy Trinity Revealed

In the Old Testament we find Yahweh, the one Lord and God, acting toward the world through His Word and His Spirit. In the New Testament the "Word becomes flesh" (Jn 1.14). As Jesus of Nazareth, the only-begotten Son of God becomes man. And the Holy Spirit, who is in Jesus making him the Christ, is poured forth from God upon all flesh (Acts 2.17).

One cannot read the Bible nor the history of the Church without being struck by the numerous references to God the Father, the Son (Word) of God and the Holy Spirit. The New Testament record, and the life of the Orthodox Church is absolutely incomprehensible and meaningless without constant affirmation of the existence, interrelation and interaction of the Father, the Son, and the Holy Spirit towards each other and towards man and the world.

Wrong Doctrines of the Trinity

The main question for the Church to answer about God is that of the relationship between the Father, the Son, and the Holy Spirit. According to Orthodox Tradition, there are a number of wrong doctrines which must be rejected.

One wrong doctrine is that the Father alone is God and that the Son and the Holy Spirit are creatures, made "from nothing" like angels, men and the world. The Church answers that the Son and the Holy Spirit are not creatures, but are uncreated and divine with the Father, and they act with the Father in the divine act of creation of all that exists.

Another wrong doctrine is that God in Himself is One God who merely appears in different forms to the world: Now as the Father, then as the Son, and still again as the Holy Spirit. The Church answers once more that the Son and Word is "in the beginning with God"(Jn 1.12) as is the Holy Spirit, and that the Three are eternally distinct. The Son is "of God" and the Spirit is "of God." The Son and the Spirit are not merely aspects of God, without, so to speak, a life and existence of their own. How strange it would be to imagine, for example, that when the Son becomes man and prays to his Father and acts in obedience to Him, it is all an illusion with no reality in fact, a sort of divine presentation played before the world with no reason or truth for it at all!

A third wrong doctrine is that God is one, and that the Son and the Spirit are merely names for relations which God has with Himself. Thus, the Thought and Speech of God is called the Son, while the Life and Action of God is called the Spirit; but in fact—in genuine actuality—there are no such "realities in themselves" as the Son of God and the Spirit of God. Both are just metaphors for mere aspects of God. Again, however, in such a doctrine the Son and the Spirit have no existence and no life of their own. They are not real, but are mere illusions.

Still another wrong doctrine is that the Father is one God, the Son is another God, and the Holy Spirit still another God. There cannot be "three gods," says the Church, and certainly not "gods" who are created or made. Still less can there be "three gods" of whom the Father is "higher" and the others "lower." For there to be more than one God, or "degrees of divinity" are both contradictions which cannot be defended, either by divine revelation or by logical thinking.

Thus, the Church teaches that while there is only One God, yet there are Three who are God—the Father, the Son, and the Holy Spirit—perfectly united and never divided yet not merged into one with no proper distinction. How then does the Church defend its doctrine that God is both One and yet Three?

One God, One Father

First of all, it is the Church's teaching and its deepest experience that there is only one God because there is only one Father.

In the Bible the term "God" with very few exceptions is used primarily as a name for the Father. Thus, the Son is the "Son of God," and the Spirit is the "Spirit of God." The Son is born from the Father, and the Spirit proceeds from the Father—both in the same timeless and eternal action of the Father's own being.

In this view, the Son and the Spirit are both one with God and in no way separated from Him. Thus, the Divine Unity consists of the Father, with His Son and His Spirit distinct from Himself and yet perfectly united together in Him.

One God: One Divine Nature and Being

What the Father is, the Son and the Spirit are also. This is the Church's teaching. The Son, born of the Father, and the Spirit, proceeding from Him, share the divine nature with God, being "of one essence" with Him.

Thus, as the Father is "ineffable, inconceivable, invisible, incomprehensible, ever-existing and eternally the same" (Divine Liturgy of St John Chrysostom), so the Son and the Spirit are exactly the same. Every attribute of divinity which belongs to God the Father—life, love, wisdom, truth, blessedness, holiness, power, purity, joy—belongs equally as well to the Son and the Holy Spirit. The being, nature, essence, existence and life of God the Father, the Son and the Holy Spirit are absolutely and identically one and the same.

One God: One Divine Action and Will

Since the being of the Holy Trinity is one, whatever the Father wills, the Son and the Holy Spirit will also. What the Father does, the Son and the Holy Spirit do also. There is no will and no action of God the Father which is not at the same time the will and action of the Son and the Holy Spirit.

In Himself, in eternity, as well as towards the world in creation, revelation, incarnation, redemption, sanctification, and glorification—the will and action of the Trinity are one: from the divine Father, through the divine Son, in the divine Holy Spirit. Every action of God is the action of the Three. No one person of the Trinity acts independently of or in isolation from the others. The action of each is the action of all; the action of all is the action of each. And the divine action is essentially one.

One God: One Divine Knowledge and Love

Since each person of the Trinity is one with the others, each knows the same Truth and exercises the same Love. The knowledge of each is the knowledge of all, and the Love of each is the Love of all.

If taken in distinction, each person of the Trinity knows and loves the others with such absolute perfection, knowledge, and love that there is nothing unknown and nothing unloved of each in the others, and all in all. Thus, if the creaturely knowledge of men can unite minds in full unanimity, and if the creaturely love of men can bring the divided together into one heart and one soul and even one flesh, how incomparably more perfect and absolutely uniting must be the oneness when the Knowers and Lovers are eternal and divine.

The Three Divine Persons

In Orthodox terminology the Father, the Son and the Holy Spirit are called three divine **persons**. **Person** is defined here simply as the **subject of existence and life**—hypostasis in the traditional church language.

As the being, essence or nature of a reality answers the question "what?", the **person** of a reality answers the question "which one?" or "who?" Thus, when we ask "What is God?" we answer that God is the divine, perfect, eternal, absolute . . . and when we ask "Who is God?" we answer that God is the Father, the Son, and the Holy Spirit.

The saints of the Church have explained this tri-unity of God by using such an example from worldly existence. We see three men. "What are they?" we ask. "They are human beings," we answer. Each is man, possessing the same humanity and the same human nature defined in a certain way: created, temporal, physical, rational, etc. In **what** they are, the three men are one. But in **who** they are, they are three, each absolutely unique and distinct from the others. Each man in his own unique way is distinctly a man. One man is not the other, though each man is still human with one and the same human nature and form.

Turning to God, we may ask in the same way: "**What** is it?" In reply we say that it is God defined as absolute perfection: "ineffable, inconceivable, invisible, incomprehensible, ever-existing, and eternally the same." We then ask, "**Who** is it?", and we answer that it is the Trinity : Father, Son, and Holy Spirit. In who God is, there are three persons who are each absolutely unique and distinct. Each is not the other, though each is still divine with the same divine nature and form. Therefore, while being one in **what** they are; the Father, the Son, and the Holy Spirit are Three in **who** they are. And because of **what** and **who** they are—namely, uncreated, divine persons—they are undivided and perfectly united in their timeless, spaceless, sizeless, shapeless super-essential existence, as well as in their one divine life, knowledge, love, goodness, power, will, action, etc.

Thus, according to the Orthodox Tradition, it is the mystery of God that there are Three who are divine; Three who live and act by one and the same divine perfection, yet each according to his own personal distinctness and uniqueness. Thus it is said that the Father, the Son and the Holy Spirit are each divine with the same divinity, yet each in his own divine way. And as the uncreated divinity has three divine subjects, so each divine action has three divine actors; there are three divine aspects to every action of God, yet the action remains one and the same.

We discover, therefore, one God the Father Almighty with His one unique Son (Image and Word) and His one Holy Spirit. There is one living God with His one perfect divine Life, who is personally the Son, with His one Spirit of Life. There is one True God with His one divine Truth, who is personally the Son, with His one Spirit of Truth. There is one wise and loving God with His one Wisdom and Love, who is personally the Son, with His one Spirit of Wisdom and Love. The examples could go on indefinitely: the one divine Father personifying every aspect of His divinity in His one divine Son, who is personally activated by His one divine Spirit. We will see the living implications of the Trinity as we survey the activity of God in his actions toward man and the world.

The Holy Trinity in Creation

God the Father created the world through the Son (Word) in the Holy Spirit. The Word of God is present in all that exists, making it to exist by the power of the Spirit. Thus, according to Orthodox doctrine, the universe itself is a revelation of God in the Word and the Spirit. The Word is in all that exists, causing it to be, and the Spirit is in all that exists as the power of its being and life.

This is most evident in God's special creature, man. Man is made in the image of God, and so he bears within him the unique likeness of God which is eternally and perfectly expressed in the divine Son of God, the Uncreated and Absolute Image of the Father. Thus, man is "logical"; that is, he participates in God's *Logos* (the Son and Word) and so is free, knowing, loving, reflecting on the creaturely level the very nature of God as the uncreated Son does on the level of divinity.

Man also is "spiritual"; he is the special temple of God's Spirit. The Breath of God's Life is breathed into him in the most special way. Thus, among creatures man alone is empowered to imitate God and to participate in His life. Man has the competence and ability to become a Son of God, mirroring the eternal Son, reflecting the divine nature because he is inspired by the Holy Spirit as is no other creature. Thus, one saint of the Church has said that for man to be a man, he must have the Spirit of God in him. Only then can he fulfill his humanity; only then can he be made a true Son of God, likened to him who is only-begotten.

On the most basic level of creation, therefore, we see the Trinitarian dimensions of the being and action of God: the Word and the Spirit of God enter man and the world to allow them to be and to become that for which the Father has willed their existence.

The Holy Trinity in Salvation

With man's failure to fulfill himself in his created uniqueness, God undertakes the special action of salvation. The Father sends forth His Son (Word) and His Spirit in yet another mission. The Word and the Spirit come to the Old Testament saints to make known the Father. The Word, as it were, incarnates himself in the Law (in Hebrew called the "words") which is inspired by the Spirit. The Spirit inspires the prophets to proclaim the Word of God. Thus, the Law and the

Prophets are revelations of God in His Word and His Spirit. They are partial revelations, "shadows" (as the New Testament calls them), prefiguring the total revelation of the "fullness of time" and preparing its coming.

When the time is fulfilled and the world is made ready, the Word and the Spirit come once more—no longer by their mere action and power, but now in their own persons, dwelling personally in the world.

The Word becomes flesh. The only-begotten Son is born as a man, Jesus of Nazareth. And the Spirit who is in him is given to all men to make them also sons of the Father in an eternal development of attaining His perfection by growing forever "to the measure of the stature of the fullness of Christ" (Eph 4.13).

Thus, in the New Testament we have the full epiphany of God, the full manifestation of the Holy Trinity: the Father through the Son in the Spirit to us; and we in the Spirit through the Son to the Father.

The Holy Trinity in the Church

The life of the Church is the life of men in the Holy Trinity. In the Church all become one in Christ, all put on the deified humanity of the Son of God. "For as many as have been baptized into Christ have put on Christ" (Gal 3.27). The unity of the Church is the unity of many into one, the one Body of Christ, the one living temple of God, the one people and family of God.

Within the one body there are many individual members. Many "living stones" constitute the living temple. Many brothers and sisters make up the one family of which God is the Father. The unique diversity of each member of the one Body of Christ is guaranteed by the presence of the Holy Spirit. Each unique person is inspired by the Spirit to be a true man, a true son of God in his own distinct way. Thus, as the Body of the Church is one in Christ, the one Holy Spirit gives to each member the possibility of fulfilling himself in God and so of being one with all others in calling God "Father" (See 1 Cor 12).

The Church, then, as the perfect unity of many persons into one fully united organism, is a reflection of the Trinity itself. For the Church, being many unique and distinct persons, is called to be one mind, one heart, one soul and one body in the one Truth and Love of God Himself. The calling of the Church to be one in all things is the prototype of the vocation of all mankind which was originally created by God as many persons in one nature, ultimately destined by God for ever-more-perfect growth in free unity of Truth and Love, in the life of God's Kingdom.

The Holy Trinity in the Sacraments

The sacraments of the Church portray the Trinitarian character of the life of God and man. Each person is **baptized** by the Holy Spirit into the one humanity of Christ. Being baptized, each person is given the "seal of the gift of the Holy Spirit" of God in **chrismation** to be a "christ", i.e. an anointed son of God to live the life of Christ.

In **marriage** the unity of two into one makes the new unity a reflection of the unity of the Trinity, and the unity of Christ and the Church. For the family of many persons united in one truth and love is indeed the created manifestation of the one family of God's Kingdom, and of God Himself, the Blessed Trinity.

In **penance** once more we renew our new life as sons of the Father through the grace of Christ by the power of the Holy Spirit, forgiven and reunited into the unity of God in His Church.

In **holy unction** the Spirit anoints the sufferer to suffer and die in Christ and so to be healed and made alive with the Father for eternity.

The **priesthood** itself, the ministry of the Church, is nothing other than the concrete manifestation in the Church of the presence of Christ by the same Holy Spirit who makes accessible to all men the action of the Father and the way to everlasting communion in and with Him.

Finally, the "mystery of mysteries," the **Holy Eucharist**, is the actual experience of all Christian people led to communion with God the Father by the power of the Holy Spirit through Christ the Son who is present in the Word of the Gospel and in the Passover Meal of His Body and Blood eaten in remembrance of Him. The very movement of the Divine Liturgy—towards the Father through Christ the Word and the Lamb, in the power of the Holy Spirit—is the living sacramental symbol of our eternal movement in and toward God, the Blessed Trinity.

Even Christian prayer is the revelation of the Trinity, accomplished within the third person of the Godhead. Inspired by the Holy Spirit, men can call God "our Father" only because of the Son who has taught them and enabled them to do so. Thus, the true prayer of Christians is not the calling out of our souls in earthly isolation to a far-away God. It is the prayer in us of the divine Son of God made to His Father, accomplished in us by the Holy Spirit who himself is also divine.

> For we have received the Spirit of adoption, whereby we cry Abba! Father! The Spirit itself bears witness that we are children of God . . . for we know not what we should pray for as we ought; but the Spirit itself intercedes for us . . . (Rom 8.15–16, 26).

The Holy Trinity in Christian Life

The new commandment of Christian life is "to be perfect as your heavenly Father is perfect" (Mt 5.48). It is to love as Christ himself has loved. "This is my commandment, that you love one another as I have loved you" (Jn 15.12). Men cannot live the Christian life of divine love in imitation of God's perfection without the grace of the Holy Spirit.

With the power of God, however, what is impossible to men becomes possible. "For with God all things are possible" (Mk 10.27).

The Christian life is the life of God accomplished in men by the Spirit of Christ. Men can live as Christ has lived, doing the things that he did and becoming sons of God in Him by the power of the Holy Spirit. Thus, once more, the Christian life is a Trinitarian life.

By the Holy Spirit given by God through Christ, men can share the life, the love, the truth, the freedom, the goodness, the holiness, the wisdom, the knowledge of God Himself. It is this conviction and experience which has caused the development in the Orthodox Church of the affirmation of the fact that the essence of Christianity is "the acquisition of the Holy Spirit" and the "deification" of man by the grace of God, the so-called **theosis**.

The saints of the Church are unanimous in their claim that Christian life is the participation in the life of the Blessed Trinity in the most genuine and realistic way. It is the life of men becoming divine. In the smallest aspects of everyday life Christians are called to live the life of God the Father, which is communicated to them by Christ, the Son of God, and made possible for them by the Holy Spirit who lives and acts within them.

The Holy Trinity in Eternal Life

At the end of the ages Christ will come in the glory of God the Father, He will make the Father known throughout all creation. The Holy Spirit will fill all things and enable all to be in union with God through Christ for eternity. Again we have the presence and action of the Holy Trinity.

What we know and experience now in the world as members of the Church will be manifested in power in the life of the kingdom to come. The essence of life everlasting is the life of the Holy Trinity, the same eternal life given to us already in the mystery of faith.

And I saw no temple in the city, for the Lord God Almighty and the Lamb [Christ] are the temple of it. And the city had no need of the sun . . . for the glory of God did lighten it, and the Lamb [Christ] is the light thereof . . .

And the throne of God and the Lamb [Christ] shall be in it, and his servants shall see him . . . and they shall see his face . . .

And the Spirit and the Bride [the Church] say Come!

(Rev 21.22; 22.3, 17)

In the eternal life of the Kingdom of God, the Holy Trinity will fill all creation: the Father through the Son in the Holy Spirit. Every man enlightened by Christ in the Spirit will know the invisible Father. "And this is eternal life, that they may know thee the only true God, and Jesus Christ whom thou hast sent" (Jn 17.3). Such knowledge is possible only by the indwelling of the Spirit of God, "the fullness of Him who fills all in all" (Eph 1.23; 2.22).

Come O Ye People! Let us adore the Three-Personal Godhead, the Son in the Father with the Holy Spirit.
For before all time the Father gave birth to the Son, co-eternal and co-enthroned with Himself.
And the Holy Spirit was in the Father, glorified with the Son.
Adoring One Power, One Essence, One Divinity, let us cry:
O Holy God who made all things by the Son through the cooperation of the Holy Spirit!
O Holy Mighty through whom we know the Father and through whom the Holy Spirit comes ino the world!
O Holy Immortal, the Spirit, the Comforter, who proceeds from the Father and rests in the Son!
O Most Holy Trinity! Glory to Thee!

(The Vespers of Pentecost)

144

PART II
SCRIPTURE

4

the
BIBLE

Bible

The Bible is the book of sacred writings of God's People of the Old and New Testaments.

The People of God of the Old Testament were the Jews, the descendants of Abraham, Isaac and Jacob, whose name was changed by God to **Israel** (Gen 32.28). These people are also called the **Hebrews**. They remain forever as God's chosen people for from them "according to the flesh" Christ, the Son of God, was born (Rom 9.5). This Son of God is Jesus of Nazareth, the Messiah-King of Israel and the Savior of the world (See Mt 1–2, Lk 1–2, Rom 8.3, Gal 4.4, Heb 1–5). The Old Testamental writings of the People of Israel remain forever as the Word of God for all who believe in God and wish to know His divine Truth and to do His divine Will.

The People of God of the New Testament are the **Christians**—those who believe in Jesus as "the Christ, the Son of the Living God" and who belong to the Church which He has founded upon faith in Himself (See Mt 16.13–20). The People of God of the New Testament also have their holy writings which bear witness to Christ and which are affirmed to be the Word of God.

Thus, the Bible as a book, or a collection of many books, has two main parts. It has the **Old Testament** writings which prepare the world for the coming of Christ, and, it has the **New Testament** writings which testify to the fact that Christ has come and has saved the world.

Word of God

The Bible is called the written **Word of God**. This does not mean that the Bible fell from heaven ready made. Neither does this mean that God dictated the Bible word for word to men who were merely His passive instruments. It means that God has revealed Himself as the true and living God to His People, and that as one aspect of His divine self-revelation God inspired His People to produce **scriptures**, i.e., writings which constitute the true and genuine expressions of His Truth and His Will for His People and for the whole world.

The words of the Bible are human words, for indeed, **all** words are human. They are human words, however, which God Himself inspired to be written in order to remain as the scriptural witness to Himself. As human words, the words of the Bible contain all of the marks of the men who wrote them, and of the time and the culture in which they were written. Nevertheless, in the full integrity of their human condition and form, the words of the Bible are truly the very Word of God.

The Bible is truly the Word of God in human form because its origin is not in man but in God, Who willed and inspired its creation. In this sense, the Bible is not like any other book. In the Bible, in and through the words of men, one finds the self-revelation of God and can come to a true and genuine knowledge of Him and His will and purpose for man and the world. In and through the Bible, human persons can enter into communion with God.

All scripture is inspired by God and is profitable for teaching, for reproof, for correction, and for training in righteousness, that the man of God may be complete, equipped for every good work (2 Tim 3.16–17).

It is the faith of the Orthodox Church that the Bible, as the divinely-inspired Word of God in the words of men, contains no formal errors or inner contradictions concerning the relationship between God and the world. There may be incidental inaccuracies of a non-essential character in the Bible. But the eternal spiritual and doctrinal message of God, presented in the Bible in many different ways, remains perfectly consistent, authentic, and true.

Authorship

The Bible has many different human authors. Some books of the Bible do not indicate in any way who wrote them. Other books bear the names of persons to whom authorship is ascribed. In some cases it is perfectly clear that the indicated author is in fact the person who actually wrote the book with his own hands. In other cases it is as clear that the author of the book had another person do the actual writing of his work in the manner of a secretary. In still other cases it is the Tradition of the Church, and not seldom the opinion of biblical scholars, that the indicated author of a given book of the Bible is not the person (or persons) who wrote it, but the person who originally inspired its writing, whose name is then attached to it as its author.

In a number of instances the Tradition of the Church is not clear about the authorship of certain books of the Bible, and in many cases biblical scholars present innumerable theories about authorship which they then debate among themselves. It is impossible to establish the authorship of any book of the Bible by scholarship, however, since historical and literary studies are relative by nature.

Because the Orthodox Church teaches that the entire Bible is inspired by God Who in this sense is its one original author, the Church Tradition considers the identity of the human authors as incidental to the correct interpretation and proper significance of the books of the Bible for the believing community. In no case would the Church admit that the identity of the author determines the authenticity or validity of a book which is viewed as part of the Bible, and under no circumstances would it be admitted that the value or the proper understanding and use of any book of the Bible in the Church depends on the human writer alone.

Interpretation

The Bible is the book of sacred writings for God's People, the Church. It was produced in the Church, by and for the Church, under divine inspiration as an essential part of the total reality of God's covenant relationship with His People. It is the authentic Word of God for those who belong to God's chosen assembly of believers, to the Israel of old and to the Church of Christ today and forever.

The Bible lives in the Church. It comes alive in the Church and has the most profound divine meaning for those who are members of the community which God has established, in which He dwells, and to which, through His Word and His Spirit, He has given Himself for participation, communion and life everlasting. Outside of the total life and experience of the community of faith, which is the Church of Christ, "the pillar and bulwark of the truth" (1 Tim 3.15) no one can truly understand and correctly interpret the Bible.

> *First of all you must understand that no prophecy of scripture is a matter of one's own interpretation, because no prophecy came by the impulse of man, but men moved by the Holy Spirit spoke from God* (2 Pet 1.20).

Scholars of the Bible can help men to understand its divine contents and meaning. Through their archeological, historical, and literary studies they can offer much light to the words of the scriptures. But by themselves and by their academic work alone, no men can produce the proper interpretation of the Bible. Only Christ, the living and personal Word of God, Who comes from the Father and lives in His Church through the Holy Spirit, can make God known and can give the right understanding of the scriptural Word of God.

> *In the beginning was the Word, and the Word was with God and the Word was God. . . . And the Word became flesh and dwelt among us, full of grace and truth. . . . For the law was given through Moses; grace*

and truth came through Jesus Christ. No one has ever seen God; the only-begotten Son, who is in the bosom of the Father, He has made Him known (Jn 1.1–18).

Jesus Christ, the Word of God in human flesh, alone makes God known. And Jesus, besides being Himself the living incarnation of God, the living fulfillment of the law and the prophets (Mt 5.17), is also the One by whom the Bible is rightly interpreted.

And [being risen from the dead] he said to them, "O foolish men and slow of heart to believe all that the prophets have spoken. Was it not necessary that the Christ should suffer these things and enter into his glory?"

And beginning with Moses and all the prophets, he interpreted to them in all the scriptures the things concerning himself (Lk 24.25–27).

And he said to them, "These are my words which I spoke to you, while I was still with you, that everything written about me in the law of Moses and the prophets and the psalms must be fulfilled." Then he opened their minds to understand the scriptures. . . . (Lk 24.44–45; also Jn 5.45–47).

Jesus Christ remains forever in His Church by the Holy Spirit to open men's minds to understand the Bible (Jn 14.26, 16.13). Only within Christ's Church, in the community of faith, of grace, and of truth, can men filled with the Holy Spirit understand the meaning and purpose of the Bible's holy words. Thus, speaking about those who do not believe in Jesus as the Messiah, the apostle Paul contends that when they read the Bible a "veil" hides its true meaning from them "because only through Christ is it taken away" (2 Cor 3.14).

Yes, to this day whenever Moses is read a veil lies over their minds; but when a man turns to the Lord, the veil is removed. Now the Lord is the

Spirit, and where the Spirit of the Lord is, there is freedom. And we
all [i.e. believers in Christ] with unveiled face, beholding the glory of
the Lord, are being changed into his likeness from one degree of glory
to another; for this comes from the Lord who is the Spirit. Therefore,
. . . we refuse to practice cunning or to tamper with God's word, but
by the open statement of the truth we would commend ourselves to
every man's conscience in the sight of God. And even if our gospel is
veiled, it is veiled only to those who are perishing. In their case the god
of this world has blinded the minds of the unbelievers, to keep them
from seeing the light of the glory of Christ, who is the likeness of God
(2 Cor 3.15–4.4).

In the New Testament, Christ not only provides the correct interpretation of the Bible, He also allows the believers themselves to be
directly enlightened by the Holy Spirit and to be themselves "the letter
from Christ. … written not with ink, but with the Spirit of the living
God, not on tablets of stone, but on tablets of human hearts" (2 Cor
3.3). Thus is fulfilled the prediction of the old covenant that in the
time of the Messiah "they all shall be taught of God" by direct divine
inspiration and instruction (Jn 6.45, Is 54.13, Ezek 36.26, Jer 31.31,
Joel 2.28, Mic 4.2, et al.). It is only within the living Tradition of the
Church under the direct inspiration of Christ's Spirit that the proper
interpretation of the Bible can be made.

5

OLD TESTAMENT

Law

The first part of the Bible is called the **Torah**, which means the Law. It is also called the **Pentateuch** which means the **five books**. These books are also called the **Books of Moses**. They include Genesis, Exodus, Leviticus, Numbers, and Deuteronomy. The events described in these books, from the calling of Abraham to the death of Moses, probably took place sometime in the second millennium before Christ (2000–1200 BC).

The Book of **Genesis** contains the pre-history of the **people of Israel**. It begins with the story of the creation of the world, the fall of Adam and Eve and the subsequent, quite sinful, history of the

children of Adam. It then tells of God's call and promise of salvation to **Abraham**, and the story of **Isaac** and **Jacob**, whom God named **Israel**, ending with the settlement of the twelve tribes of Israel—the families of the twelve sons of Jacob—in Egypt, during the time of Joseph's favor with the Egyptian Pharaoh. In traditional Church language, Abraham, Isaac, and Jacob are called the **patriarchs**.

The Book of **Exodus** relates the deliverance of the people of Israel by **Moses** from the slavery in Egypt to which they were subjected after the death of Joseph. It tells of the revelation of God to Moses of His divine name of **Yahweh—I AM WHO I AM** (3.14). It gives the account of the passover and the exodus, and the journey of the Israelites, led by God, through the desert. Also, in this book is the narrative of God's gift of the Ten Commandments to Moses on Mount Sinai, and the other laws which God gave to Moses concerning the moral and ritual conduct of His People.

The Book of **Leviticus** is a further book of laws, primarily concerned with the priestly and ritual offices of the people which were conducted by men taken from the tribe of Levi.

The Book of **Numbers** concerns itself primarily with a census of the people. It also contains laws given by God to Moses, and further narratives about the movement of God's People through the wilderness to the land which God promised them.

The Book of **Deuteronomy**, which means the "second law," is again primarily a law code in which is told again the story of the Ten Commandments and the institution of the Mosaic laws of moral and ritual conduct. It ends with Moses' blessing of the people, and his vision of the promised land into which Joshua would lead God's People after his death, the account of which ends the **Books of Moses**.

Scholars tell us that the Law was not written by the personal hand of Moses and that the books show evidence of being the result of a number of oral and written traditions transmitted among the People of Israel, containing material of later periods. Nevertheless, in the Tradition of Israel and of the Christian Church, the Law remains essentially connected with Moses, the great man of God to whom "the Lord used to speak . . . face to face, as a man speaks to his friend" (Ex 33.11).

The Ten Commandments

 i I am the LORD your God, who brought you out of the land of Egypt, out of the house of bondage. You shall have no other gods before me.

 ii You shall not make for yourself a graven image, or any likeness of anything that is in heaven above. or that is in the earth beneath, or that is in the water under the earth. You shall not bow down to them or serve them: for I the LORD your God am a jealous God, visiting the iniquity of the fathers upon the children to the third and fourth generation of those who hate me, but showing steadfast love to thousands of those who love me and keep my commandments.

 iii You shall not take the name of the LORD your God in vain; for the LORD will not hold him guiltless who takes his name in vain.

 iv Remember the sabbath day, to keep it holy. Six days you shall labor, and do all your work: but the seventh day is a sabbath to the LORD your God; in it you shall not do any work, you, or your son, or your daughter, your manservant, or your maidservant, or your cattle, or the sojourner who is within your gates; for in six days the LORD made heaven and earth. the sea. and all that is in them, and rested the seventh day; therefore, the LORD blessed the sabbath day and hallowed it.

 v Honor your father and your mother, that your days may be long in the land which the Lord your God gives you.

 vi You shall not kill.

 vii You shall not commit adultery.

 viii You shall not steal.

 ix You shall not bear false witness against your neighbor.

 x You shall not covet your neighbor's house; you shall not covet your neighbor's wife, or his man servant, or his maidservant, or his ox. or his ass, or anything that is your neighbor's.

(Ex 20.1–17)

History

Following the Law in the Bible are those books which are called **historical**. They cover the history of Israel from the settlement in the promised land of Canaan to the first centuries before Christ. They include Joshua, Judges, Ruth, 1 and 2 Samuel, 1 and 2 Kings, 1 and 2 Chronicles, Ezra, Nehemiah, and Esther, as well as 1 and 2 Esdras, Tobit, Judith, and 1 and 2 Maccabees, which in the English Bible includes 3 Maccabees.

In the biblical listing of the Orthodox Church, which is generally that of the **Septuagint**, the Greek translation of the Hebrew Bible, 1 and 2 Samuel are called 1 and 2 Kings, and 1 and 2 Kings are called 3 and 4 Kings. Also, the so-called **apocryphal** books, listed above after Esther, are considered by the Orthodox as genuine parts of the Bible. The Old Testament apocrypha is a body of writings considered by the non-Orthodox to be of close association with the Bible, but not actually part of its official canonical contents.

The Book of **Joshua** begins with the People of Israel crossing over the Jordan River and into the promised land led by Joshua, the successor of Moses. It tells of the victories of the Israelites over the local inhabitants, and the settlement of the twelve tribes in the territories appointed to each by Moses.

The Book of **Judges** tells of the period when the Israelites were ruled by the "judges" whom God appointed, the most famous being Ehud, Deborah, Gideon, Jephthah, and Samson. During this period, the Israelites were often unfaithful to God and given to evil. They were constantly at war with themselves and their neighbors. The book ends with the line: "In those days there was no king in Israel; every man did what was right in his eyes" (Judg 23.25).

The Book of **Ruth** is a very short story of the Moabite woman whom God blessed to be the wife of Boaz, the great-grandmother of David the King.

The books of **Samuel** and **Kings** begin with the birth of **Samuel**, the prophet whom God chose to anoint **Saul** as the first king of Israel. Until Saul there was no king, for God Himself was to be King for His People. Yet Israel wished to be "like all the nations" and God yielded, with reluctance, to their desires (Sam 8). Saul soon became evil and God sent Samuel to anoint **David**, the shepherd boy, as king in his place. Saul was enraged and made war against David, but David was merciful to him though he could easily have killed him. During this whole time, the Israelites were constantly at war. Saul finally killed himself rather than be taken in battle, and David became the only king. Having subdued all of his enemies, both within Israel and without, David established a glorious kingdom centered in **Jerusalem**, the city which he built. David's son, **Solomon**, favored by God with great wisdom, enlarged his father's kingdom and built the great **temple** for God on Mount Zion. The kingship of David and Solomon lasted from 1000–422 BC.

No sooner had Solomon died, than the kingdom collapsed. Two rival states emerged, **Israel** and **Judah**, which were constantly at war with each other and with those around them. This was a time of great decadence and evil that lasted for about three hundred years and ended with the **Babylonian Captivity** (587–539 BC). It was the time of **Elijah** and many of the great prophets of God.

Babylon was captured by the Persians led by Cyrus and Darius who restored the Israelites to their homeland. The books of **Ezra** and **Nehemiah** tell of the resettlement of the Jews, and of the rebuilding and the reopening of the temple in Jerusalem.

The two books of **Chronicles** date from this same period and may well have been compiled by Ezra, although scholars consider them as the work of third century authors, perhaps the same who wrote Ezra and Nehemiah. The Chronicles cover the history of Israel from Adam to the time of Cyrus. They contain numerous genealogies, and show particular interest in David and the Kings as well as in the temple and the priesthood. In the Septuagint Bible the Chronicles are called **Para-lipomena** which means "that which has been left out," thus indicating their purpose as being to fill in what has been excluded from the earlier historical books of the Bible.

The Book of **Esther**, and those of **1** and **2 Esdras**, **Tobit**, **Judith**, and **1** and **2 Maccabees** which, as we have said, are included in the Bible in the Orthodox Church, bring the history of Israel down to New Testament times. They tell of the reorganization of the Jewish community around the temple, the cult and the law as a mere remnant of the great nation, or nations of Israel and Judah, which existed before the time of exile; a struggling remnant constantly in subjugation to external powers. It is mostly the case that the historical books of the Bible were written well after the events described in them actually took place.

Wisdom

The books of the Bible which are commonly called the **Wisdom books** include Job, Psalms, Proverbs, Ecclesiastes, and the Song of Solomon, as well as the Wisdom of Jesus, Son of Sirach, also called Ecclesiasticus, and the Wisdom of Solomon from the so-called apocrypha.

The Book of **Job**, usually dated sometime at the period of exile, is the story of righteous suffering in which the sufferer pleads his cause before God only to "repent in dust and ashes" (42.6) upon seeing the Lord for himself and being confronted by Him with His own defense of His unspeakable and unfathomable majesty. Selections from this book are read on the first days of Holy Week in the Orthodox Church because they deal with the most profound problem facing believers, the problem of suffering, which is brought to its ultimate completion in Christ who is not merely the most perfect of "suffering innocents," but indeed the Suffering God in human flesh.

The Book of **Proverbs**, called the "proverbs of Solomon," undoubtedly comes from Solomon's time, although scholars place some of the proverbs at a much later date and tell us that the book was put in its present form only after the Babylonian exile. The proverbs are short sayings concerning the proper conduct of wise and righteous persons. They are read in their entirety at t he weekday Vesper services of the Church during Great Lent. Selections from the Proverbs are also read at the vigils of a number of feasts of the Church since for Christians the **Wisdom of God** is personified and embodied in Christ.

Ecclesiastes is a book of common-sense meditations on the vanity of life in this world and the wisdom of fearing God and keeping His commandments which is "the whole duty of man" (11.3). It is traditionally ascribed to Solomon, the Preacher. Scholars place the book in the third century before Christ, however, and find in its message a hellenistic spirit taken over by the Jews in diaspora among the gentile nations.

The same hellenistic spirit and influences of Greek philosophy, but to a much greater degree, are found in both the **Wisdom of Jesus, Son of Sirach** and the **Wisdom of Solomon** which come from the same period, the very eve of New Testament times. Of the three books just mentioned, only the Wisdom of Solomon, which is considered to be the last of them written, is read liturgically in the Orthodox Church.

The **Song of Solomon**—also called the **Song of Songs** or **Canticle of Canticles**—is considered by scholars as a Canaanite wedding hymn of uncertain date. In Orthodox Church Tradition it is interpreted as a mystical love story between man's soul and God. Christian saints of East and West, such as Gregory of Nyssa and Bernard of Clairvaux, have given such a meaning to the book which is in line with the biblical tradition of viewing the interrelationship of God and His People as that of conjugal love (See Hos, Jer 2–3, Eph 5, Rev 21–22). This book is never read in the liturgical services of the Orthodox Church, although certain lines from it are traditionally sung in the Russian Orthodox Church when the bride approaches her bridegroom in the church before the celebration of their marriage.

Although not technically a "wisdom" book, mention may be made at this point of **The Prayer of Manasseh** from the so-called apocrypha. This penitential prayer of the King of Judah, which for the Orthodox is part of the Bible, is included in the **Great Compline** service of the Orthodox Church.

Psalms

The **Psalms** are the divinely-inspired songs of the People of Israel. They are traditionally called the "psalms of David," although many of them most certainly come from other authors of much later times. The enumeration and the wording of the psalms differ in various scriptural traditions. The Orthodox Church follows the **Septuagint** version of the psalter and for this reason the numbers and not seldom the texts of certain psalms are different in Orthodox service books from what they are in the Bibles which are translated from the Hebrew.

In the Orthodox Church, the entire psalter is divided into twenty sections and is chanted each week in those monasteries and churches which perform the entire liturgical office. Various psalms and verses of psalms are used in all liturgical services of the Orthodox Church (see *Worship*).

Virtually all states of man's soul before God are found expressed in the psalms: praising, thanking, blessing, rejoicing, petitioning, repenting, lamenting, questioning and even complaining. Many of the psalms are centered in the cultic rituals of the Jerusalem temple and the Davidic kingship. Others recount God's saving actions in Israelite history. Still others carry prophetic utterances about events yet to come, particularly those of the messianic age. Thus, for example, we find Christ quoting Psalm 8 in reference to His triumphal entry into Jerusalem; Psalm 110 in reference to his own mysterious divinity; and Psalm 22, when, hanging upon the cross, He cries out with the words of the psalm in which is described His crucifixion and his ultimate salvation of the world (See Mt 21.16, 22.44, 27.46).

In the Orthodox Church all of the psalms are understood as having their deepest and most genuine spiritual meaning in terms of Christ and His mission of eternal salvation. Thus, for example, the psalms which refer to the king are sung in the Church in reference to Christ's exaltation and glorification at the right hand of God. The psalms which refer to Israel's deliverance are sung in reference to Christ's redemption of the whole world. The psalms calling for victory over the enemies in battle refer to the only real Enemy, the devil, and all of his wicked works which Christ has come to destroy. Babylon thus signifies the realm of Satan, and Jerusalem, the eternal Kingdom of God. The psalms which lament the innocent suffering of the righteous are sung as the plea of the Lord Himself and all those with Him who are the "poor and needy" who will rise up to rule the earth on the day of God's terrible judgment. Thus, the psalter remains forever as the divinely-inspired song book of prayer and worship for all of God's People, and most especially for those who belong to the Messiah whose words the psalms are in their deepest and most divine significance.

Liturgical Division of the Psalter (**Kathisma**)

1	Psalms 1–8	11	Psalms 78–85
2	Psalms 9–17	12	Psalms 86–91
3	Psalms 18–24	13	Psalms 92–101
4	Psalms 25–32	14	Psalms 102–105
5	Psalms 33–37	15	Psalms 106–109
6	Psalms 38–46	16	Psalms 110–118
7	Psalms 47–55	17	Psalm 119
8	Psalms 56–64	18	Psalms 120–134
9	Psalms 65–70	19	Psalms 135–143
10	Psalms 71–77	20	Psalms 144–150

Prophets

There are sixteen books in the Bible called by the names of the prophets although not necessarily written by their hands. A **prophet** is one who speaks by the direct inspiration of God; only secondarily does the word mean one who foretells the future. Four of the prophetic books are those of the so-called **major prophets**: Isaiah, Jeremiah, Ezekiel and Daniel.

Most scholars believe that the book of **Isaiah** is the work of more than one author. It covers the period from the middle of the eighth century before Christ to the time of the Babylonian exile. It tells of the impending doom upon the people of God for their wickedness and infidelity to the Lord. And it foretells the mercy of God upon His People, as well as the gentiles, in the time of His redemption in the messianic age. The famous vision of the prophet in chapter six is included in the eucharistic prayers of the Orthodox Church. Of central importance in Isaiah are the prophecies in the first part of the book, especially chapters six to twelve, concerning the coming of the Messiah-King; and the prophecies at the end of the book, about the salvation of all creation in the **suffering servant** of the Lord. The entire book of Isaiah is read in the Church during Great Lent, and many selections are read at the vigils of the great feasts of the Church. In the New Testament scriptures there are innumerable quotations of the prophecy of Isaiah made in reference to John the Baptist, and most especially to Christ Himself.

The book of **Jeremiah** covers the period of the seventh century before Christ and, like Isaiah, prophecies the Lord's wrath upon His sinful people. Jeremiah, a most reluctant prophet, suffered greatly at the hands of the people and was constantly persecuted for his proclamation of the Word of the Lord. The book is referred to many times in the New Testament. The messianic prophecies of salvation in Jeremiah are often read in the festal services of the Church. The books of **Baruch** and the **Letter of Jeremiah** from the apocrypha go together with this prophetic book in the Orthodox version of the Bible.

The book of **Ezekiel**, who was a priest as well as a prophet, is dated at the time of the Babylonian Captivity. Once again, the prophet is directly concerned with God's righteous anger over the sins of His People, making specific reference to the presence—and the departure—of the Lord's glory in the Jerusalem Temple. Ezekiel, however, like all of the prophets, is not without hope in the mercy of God. The moving passage about God's resurrection of the "dry bones" of dead

Israel through the breathing in of His Holy Spirit is read over the tomb of Christ at the Great Saturday service of the Orthodox Church.

The prophecy of **Daniel**, read in the Church at the vigil of Easter, is concerned with the faithfulness of the Jews to their God in the time of forced apostasy. Scholars consider this book among the latest written in the Old Testament, much after the time of the Babylonian captivity in which the story is placed. Central among the book's messages is the redemption of Israel in the victorious coming of the heavenly **Son of Man**, who, in the New Testament, is identified with Christ. It is the **apocalyptic** character of the book—apocalyptic meaning that which refers to the final revelation of God and His ultimate judgment over all creation— which accounts for the placement of Daniel at a date close to New Testament times. The Song of the Three Youths which goes together with Daniel and which is placed by the non-Orthodox among the apocryphal writings, forms a genuine part of the Bible in the Orthodox Church, as do the books of **Susanna** and **Bel and the Dragon**, also part of Daniel. The Song of the Youths is part of the matinal office in the Orthodox Church.

Among the books of the so-called minor prophets, **Amos** and **Hosea** are the earliest, coming, like the first part of Isaiah, from the middle of the eighth century before Christ. Amos is the great proclaimer of the justice of God against the injustices of His People. Hosea tells of the unwavering love of God which will ultimately triumph over the adulterous harlotry of His People who unfaithfully lust after false gods.

The book of **Micah** dates from approximately the same period and is very similar in content to Isaiah. In **Micah** is found the prophecy of the Savior's birth in Bethlehem (5.2–4).

Nahum, Habakkuk, and **Zephaniah** are dated in the later part of the seventh century before Christ. They imitate Jeremiah, prophesying the wrath of a good and just God upon a wicked and unjust people. Like Jeremiah, they also foretell the restoration of Israel by the merciful Lord.

Haggai, Zechariah, Malachi, and perhaps **Obadiah,** belong to the period of the return of God's People from exile. Zechariah is famous for the oracle of the appearance of the Savior-King, "triumphant and victorious as he is, humble and riding on an ass . . ." (9.9) which referred to Christ's triumphal entry into Jerusalem on Palm Sunday. Malachi, who is ferocious against the sins of the priests, is the last of the prophets before John the Baptist whose coming he foretells, as did the others, to usher in the "great and terrible day of the Lord" (3.1, 4.5) when "the Sun of Righteousness shall arise with healing in his wings" (4.2), a reference made, according to Christians, explicitly to their Lord.

The prophecy of **Joel,** quoted by St Peter in reference to the coming of the Holy Spirit on the day of Pentecost (Acts 2), belongs to the apocalyptic style of Daniel as it speaks of the final acts of God in the days of the Lord's "great and terrible" appearance when He will execute justice and restore the fortunes of His People, delivering "all who call upon the name of the Lord" (2.31–32).

The book of **Jonah** is most likely a prophetic allegory intended to foretell the Lord's salvation of the gentiles in the time of His final messianic presence in the world. It was probably written in post-exilic times. It is read in its entirety in the Church at the Easter vigil of Great Saturday as it was directly referred to by Christ Himself as the sign of His messianic mission in the world (Mt 12.38, Lk 11.29).

It must be mentioned at this point, that the variation in names found in English for the prophets, as well as for other persons and places in the scriptures, comes from the different Hebrew and Greek language traditions of the Bible. The Orthodox sources most often tend to follow the Greek. Thus, for example, Elijah becomes Elias, Hosea becomes Osee, Habakkuk becomes Avvakum, Jonah becomes Jonas, etc. Once again we must mention as well that according to Christians, the entire Old Testament finds it deepest meaning and its most perfect fulfillment in the coming of Christ and in the life of His Church.

6

NEW TESTAMENT

Gospels

The first books of the New Testament scriptures are the four gospels of Saints Matthew, Mark, Luke and John. The word **gospel** literally means **good news** or **glad tidings**. The gospels tell of the life and teaching of Jesus, but none of them is a biography in the classical sense of the word. The gospels were not written merely to tell the story of Jesus. They were written by the disciples of Christ, who were filled with the Holy Spirit after the Lord's resurrection, to bear witness to the fact that Jesus of Nazareth is indeed the promised Messiah-Christ of Israel and the Savior of the world.

In the Orthodox Church, it is not the entire Bible, but only the book of the four gospels which is perpetually enthroned upon the altar table in the church building. This is a testimony to the fact that the life of the Church is centered in Christ, the living fulfillment of the law and the prophets, who abides perpetually in the midst of His People, the Church, through the presence of the Holy Spirit.

The gospels of Saints Matthew, Mark and Luke are called the **synoptic** gospels, which means that they "look the same". These three gospels are very similar in content and form and are most probably interrelated textually in some way, exactly how being an ongoing debate among scriptural scholars. They each were written sometime in the beginning of the second half of the first century, and the texts of each of them, as that of St John, have come down to us in Greek, the language in which they were written, with the possible exception of Matthew which may have been written originally in Aramaic, the language of Jesus.

Each of the synoptic gospels follows basically the same narrative. Each begins with Jesus' baptism by John and His preaching in Galilee. Each centers on the apostles' confession of Jesus as the promised Messiah of God, with the corresponding event of the transfiguration, and the announcement by Christ of His need to suffer and die and be raised again on the third day. And each concludes with the account of the passion, death, resurrection and ascension of the Lord.

ST MARK

The gospel of St Mark is the shortest, and perhaps the first written, of the gospels, although this is a matter of debate. Its author was not one of the twelve apostles and it is the common view that this gospel presents the "tradition" of St Peter. The gospel begins immediately with Jesus' baptism, the call of the apostles, and the preaching of Jesus accompanied by his works of forgiveness and healing. In this gospel, as in all of them, Jesus is revealed from the very beginning by His authoritative words and His miraculous works as the Holy One of God, the divine Son of Man, Who was crucified and is risen from the dead, thus bringing to the world the Kingdom of God.

ST MATTHEW

The gospel of St Matthew, who was one of the twelve apostles, is considered by some to be the earliest written gospel. There is also the opinion that it was originally written in Aramaic and not in the Greek text which has remained in the Church. It is a commonly-held view that the gospel of St Matthew was written for the Jewish Christians to show from the scriptures of the Old Testament, that Jesus, the son of David, the son of Abraham, is truly the Christ, the bearer of God's Kingdom to men.

The gospel of St Matthew abounds with references to the Old Testament. It begins with the genealogy of Jesus from Abraham and the story of Christ's birth from the Virgin in Bethlehem. Then recounting the baptism of Jesus and the temptations in the wilderness, it proceeds to the call of the disciples and the preaching and works of Christ.

The gospel of St Matthew contains the longest and most detailed record of Christ's teachings in the so-called **Sermon on the Mount** (5–7). Generally, in the Orthodox Church, it is the text of the gospel of St Matthew which is used most consistently in liturgical worship, e.g., the version of the beatitudes and the Lord's Prayer. Only this gospel contains the commission of the Lord to His apostles after the resurrection, "to make disciples of all nations, baptizing them in the name of the Father, and of the Son and of the Holy Spirit" (28.19).

ST LUKE

The gospel of St Luke, who was not one of the twelve apostles but one of the original disciples, a physician known for his association with the apostle Paul, claims to be an "orderly account . . . delivered by those who from the beginning were eyewitnesses and ministers of the Word" (1.1–4). Together with the book of Acts, also written by St Luke for a certain Theophilus, this gospel forms the most complete "history" of Christ and the early Christian Church that we have.

The gospel of St Luke, alone among the four canonical gospels, has a complete account of the birth of both Jesus and John the Baptist. Traditionally, the source for these events recorded by St Luke is considered to be Mary, the mother of Christ. We must mention at this point that in addition to the four gospels called "canonical" in that they alone have been accepted by the Church as genuine witnesses to the true life and teachings of Christ, there exist many other writings from the early Christian era which tell about Jesus, and especially His childhood, which have not been accepted by the Church as authentic and true. These writings are often called **apocryphal** (not to be confused with the so-called **apocrypha** of the Old Testament), or the **pseudoepigrapha** which literally means "false writings."

St Luke's gospel is noted for the detail of its narrative, and especially for its record of Christ's great concern for the poor and for the sinful. Certain parables warning against the dangers of riches and self-righteousness, and revealing the great mercy of God to sinners, are found only in the gospel of St Luke, for example, those of the publican and the pharisee, the prodigal son, and Lazarus and the rich man, There is also a very great emphasis in this gospel on the Kingdom of God which Christ has brought to the world and which He gives to those who continue with Him in His sufferings.

The post-resurrection account of the Lord's presence to the two disciples on the road to Ernmaeus in which only one of the disciples is named, an account found only in St Luke's gospel, gives rise to the tradition that the unnamed disciple was Luke himself.

ST JOHN

The gospel of St John is very different from the synoptic gospels. It is undoubtedly the latest written, being the work of the beloved disciple and apostle of the Lord at the end of his life near the close of the first century. In most Orthodox versions of the Bible, this gospel is printed before the others as it is the one which is first read in the Church's lectionary beginning at the divine Liturgy on Easter night.

The gospel of St John begins with its famous prologue which identifies Jesus of Nazareth with the divine Word of God of the Old Testament, the Word of God Who was "in the beginning with God," Who

"is God," the One through Whom "all things were made"(1.1–3). This Word of God "became flesh," and as Jesus, the Son of God, He makes God known to men and grants to all who believe in Him the power of partaking of His own fulness of grace and truth and of becoming themselves "children of God" (1.14ff).

From the first pages of this gospel, following the prologue, in the account of Jesus' baptism and His calling of the apostles, Jesus is presented as God's only begotten Son, the Messiah and the Lord. Throughout the gospel, He is identified as well, in various ways, with the God of the Old Testament, receiving the dd vine name of **I AM** together with the **Yahweh** of Moses and the prophets and psalms.

The gospel of St John, following the prologue, may be divided into two main parts. The first part is the so-called book of "signs," the record of a number of Jesus' miracles with detailed "commentary" about their significance in signifying Him as Messiah and Lord (2–11). Because the "signs" all have a deeply spiritual and sacramental significance for believers in Christ, with almost all of them dealing with water, wine, bread, light, the salvation of the nations, the separation from the synagogue, the forgiveness of sins, the healing of infirmities and the resurrection of the dead, it is sometimes thought that the gospel of St John was expressly written as a "theological gospel" for those who were newly initiated into the life of the Church through the sacramental mysteries of baptism, the gift of the Holy Spirit, and the eucharist. In any case, because of the contents of the book of "signs," as well as the long discourses of Christ about His relationship to God the Father, the Holy Spirit and the members of His faithful flock, in the latter part of the gospel, the apostle and evangelist John has traditionally been honored in the Church with the title of **The Theologian**.

The latter half of St John's gospel concerns the passion of Christ and its meaning for the world (11–21). Here most explicitly, in long discourses coming from the mouth of the Lord Himself, the doctrines of Christ's person and work are most deeply explained. As we have just mentioned, here Christ relates Himself to God the Father, to the Holy Spirit and to His community of believers in clear and certain terms. He is one with God, Who as Father is greater than He, Whose words He speaks, Whose works He accomplishes and Whose will He performs. And through the Holy Spirit, Who proceeds from the Father to bear witness to Him in the world, He remains abiding forever in those who are His through their faith and co-service of God.

The account of the passion in St John's gospel differs slightly from that of the synoptic gospels and is considered by many, in this instance, to be a certain clarification or correction. There are also accounts of the resurrection given which are recorded only in this gospel. The final chapter of the book is traditionally considered to be an addition following the first ending of the gospel, to affirm the reinstatement of the apostle Peter to the leadership of the apostolic community after his three denials of the Lord at the time of His passion. It may have been a necessary inclusion to offset a certain lack of confidence in St Peter by some members of the Church.

In the Tradition of the Orthodox Church, a tradition often expressed in the Church's iconography, the four gospels are considered to be symbolized in the images of the "four living creatures" of the biblical apocalypse, the lion, the ox, the man and the eagle, with the most classical interpretation connecting Matthew with the man, Luke with the ox, Mark with the lion and John with the eagle (Ezek 1.10, Rev 4.7). The four gospels, taken together, but each with its own unique style and form, remain forever as the scriptural center of the Orthodox Church.

Acts of the Apostles

The book of the **Acts of the Apostles** was written by St Luke toward the end of the first century, as the second part of his history for Theophilus about Christ and His Church. The book begins with an account of the Lord's ascension and the election of Matthias to take the place of Judas as a member of the twelve apostles. Then follows the record of the events of the day of Pentecost when the promised Holy Spirit came upon the disciples of Christ empowering them to preach the gospel of new life in the resurrected Savior to the people of Jerusalem.

The first chapters of the book tell the story of the first days of the Church in Jerusalem and provide us with a vivid picture of the primitive Christian community being built up through the work of the apostles. It tells of the people being baptized and endowed with the gift of the Holy Spirit through repentance and faith in Christ, and continuing steadfast in their devotion "to the apostles' doctrine and fellowship (communion), to the breaking of the bread and the prayers" (2.42).

Following the description of the martyrdom of the deacon Stephen, the first to give his life for Christ, **Acts** tells of the conversion of the persecutor Saul into the zealous apostle Paul, and records the events by which the first gentiles were brought into the Church by the direct action of God. There then follows an account of the first missionary activities of Saints Paul and Barnabas, and the famous fifteenth chapter in which the first council of the Church in Jerusalem is described, the council which established the conditions under which the gentiles could enter the Church relative to the Mosaic law which all of the Jewish Christians were then keeping.

The final half of the book describes the missionary activities of the apostle Paul through Syria and Cilicia, into Macedonia and Greece and back again through Ephesus to Jerusalem. It then gives the account of Saint Paul's arrest in Jerusalem, and his defense before the authorities there. The book ends with the description of Saint Paul's journey to Rome for trial, closing with the information that "he lived there two whole years . . . preaching the Kingdom of God and teaching about the Lord quite openly and unhindered" to those who came to him in his house of arrest (28.30).

The book of the Acts of the Apostles forms the apostolic lectionary of the Church's Liturgy during the time from Easter to Pentecost. Selections from it are also read at other feasts of the Church, e.g., St Stephen's Day. It is also the custom of the Church to read the book of Acts over the tomb of Christ on Good Friday, and over the body of a deceased priest at the wake prior to his burial.

Letters of St Paul

Fourteen letters, also called epistles, which are ascribed to the apostle Paul are included in the holy scriptures of the New Testament Church. We will comment on the letters in the order in which they are normally printed in the English Bible and read in the Church's liturgical year.

ROMANS

The letter to the Romans was written by St Paul from Corinth some-time at the end of the fifties of the first century. It is one of the most formal and detailed expositions of the doctrinal teaching of St Paul that we have. It is not one of the easier parts of the scripture to understand without careful study.

In this letter, the apostle Paul writes about the relationship of the Christian faith to the unbelievers, particularly the unbelieving Jews. The apostle upholds the validity and holiness of the Mosaic law while passionately defending the doctrine that salvation comes only in Christ, by faith and by grace. He discourses powerfully about the meaning of union -with Christ through baptism and the gift of the Holy Spirit. He urges great humility on the part of the gentile Christians toward Israel, and calls with great pathos and love for the regrafting of the unbelieving Jews to the genuine community of God which is in Christ Who is Himself from Israel "**according to the flesh**" (9.5) for the sake of its salvation and that of all the world.

The end of the letter is a long exhortation concerning the proper behavior of Christians, finally closing with a long list of personal greetings from the apostle and his co-workers, including one Tertius, the actual writer of the letter, to many members of the Roman Church, urging, once more, steadfastness of faith.

The letter to the Romans is read in the Church's liturgical lectionary during the first weeks following the feast of Pentecost. Selections from it are also read on various other liturgical occasions, one of which, for example, is the sacramental liturgy of baptism and chrismation (6.3–11).

FIRST CORINTHIANS

The first Christian community in Corinth, was noted neither for its inner peace and harmony, nor for the exemplary moral behavior of its members. The two letters of St Paul to the Corinthians which we have in the New Testament, written in the mid-fifties of the first century, are filled not only with doctrinal and ethical teachings, the answers to concrete questions and problems, but also with no little scolding and chastisement by the author, as well as numerous defenses of his own apostolic authority. These letters clearly demonstrate the fact that the first Christians were not all saints, and that the early Church experienced no fewer difficulties than the Church does today or at any time in its history in the world.

After a short greeting and word of gratitude to God for the grace given to the Corinthians, the first letter begins with St Paul's appeal for unity in the Church. There are deep disagreements and dissensions among the members of the community, and the apostle urges all to be fully united in the crucified Christ, by the power of the Holy Spirit in Whom there can be no divisions at all (1–3) He then defends his apostleship generally and his fatherhood of the Corinthian Church in particular, both of which were being attacked by some members of the Church. (4) Next, he deals with the problem on sexual immorality among members of the community and the matter of their going to court before pagan judges (5–6). After this comes St Paul's counsel about Christian marriage and his advice concerning the eating of food offered to idols (7–8). Then once again he defends his apostleship, stressing the fact that he has always supported himself materially and has burdened no one.

The divisions and troubles in the Corinthian community were most concretely expressed at the eucharistic gatherings of the Church. There was general disrespect and abuse of the Body and Blood of Christ, and the practice had developed where each clique was having its own separate meal. These divisions were caused in no small part by the fact that some of the community had certain spiritual gifts, for example, that of praising God in unknown tongues, which they considered as signs of their superiority over others. There also was trouble caused by women in the Church, who were using their new freedom in Christ for disruption and disorder.

In his letter St Paul urges respect and discernment for the holy eucharist as the central realization of the unity of the Church, coming from Christ, Himself. He warns against divisions in the Church because of the various spiritual gifts, urging the absolute unity of the Church as the one body of Christ which has many members and many gifts for the edification of all. He insists on the absolute primacy and superiority of love over every virtue and gift, without which all else is made void and is destroyed. He tempers those who had the gift of praising God in strange tongues, a gift which was obviously presenting a most acute problem, and calls for the exercise of all gifts and most particularly the simple and direct teaching of the Word of ,God in the Church. He appeals to the women to maintain themselves in dress and behavior proper to Christians. And finally he insists that "**all things should be done decently and in order**" (10–14).

The first letter to the Corinthians ends with a long discourse about the meaning of the resurrection of the dead in Christ which is the center of the Christian faith and preaching. The apostle closes with an appeal for money for the poor, and promising a visit, he once again insists on the absolute necessity of strength of faith, humble service and most especially, love.

SECOND CORINTHIANS

The entire second letter of St Paul to the Corinthians is a detailed enumeration and description of his sufferings and trials in the apostolate of Christ. In this letter, the apostle once again defends himself before the Corinthians, some of whom were reacting very badly to him and to his guidance and instruction in the faith. He defends the "pain" that, he is causing these people because of his exhortations and admonitions

to them concerning their beliefs and. Behavior, and he calls them to
listen to him and to follow him in his life in Christ.

Of special interest in the second letter, in addition to the detailed
record of St Paul's activities and all that he had to bear for the gospel
of Christ, is the doctrine of the apostle concerning the relationship
of Christians with God through Christ and the Holy Spirit in the
Church. Worthy of special note also, is the apostolic teaching about
the significance of the scriptures for the Christians (3–4) and the
teaching about contributions, of money for the work of the Church.
(9)The closing line of the second letter to the Corinthians, which, like
all epistles, forms part of the Church's lectionary, is used in the divine
liturgies of the Orthodox Church during the eucharistic canon.

*The grace of our Lord Jesus Christ and the love of God (the Father),
and the communion of the Holy Spirit be with you all.* (2 Corinthians 13.14)

Saint Paul's Hymn to Love

If I speak in the tongues of men and of angels, but have not love, I am a noisy gong or a clanging cymbal. And if I have prophetic powers, and understand all mysteries and all knowledge, and if I have all faith, so as to remove mountains, but have not love, I am nothing. If I give away all I have, and if I deliver my body to be burned, but have not love, I gain nothing.

Love is patient and kind; love is not jealous or boastful; it is not arrogant or rude. Love does not insist on its own way; it is not irritable or resentful; it does not rejoice at wrong, but rejoices in the right. Love bears all things, believes all things, hopes all things, endures all things.

Love never ends; as for prophecies, they will pass away; as for tongues, they will cease; as for knowledge, it will pass away. For our knowledge is imperfect and our prophecy is imperfect; but when the perfect comes, the imperfect will pass away. When I was a child, I spoke like a child, I thought like a child, I reasoned like a child; when I became a man, I gave up childish ways. For now we see in a mirror dimly, but then face to face. Now I know in part; then I shall understand fully, even as I have been fully understood. So faith, hope, love abide, these three; but the greatest of these is love.

(1 Corinthians 13)

GALATIANS

The letter of St Paul to the Galatians, most likely the southern Galatians (Lystra, Derbe, Iconium), was sent from Antioch in the early fifties. In this most vehement epistle, the apostle Paul expresses his profound anger and distress at the fact that the Galatians, who had received the genuine gospel of Christ from him, had been seduced into practicing "another gospel" which held that man's salvation requires the ritual observance of the Old Testament law, including the practice of circumcision.

The heart of this letter to the **"foolish Galatians"** (3.1) is St Paul's uncompromising defense of the fact -that his gospel is not his but Christ's, the gospel of salvation not by the law, but by grace and faith in the crucified Savior Who gives the Holy Spirit to all who believe. The apostle stresses the fact that in Christ and the Spirit there is freedom from slavery to the flesh, slavery to the elemental spirits of the universe, and slavery to the ritual requirements of the law through which no one can be saved. For the true **"Israel of God"** (6.16) in Christ and the Spirit, there is perfect freedom, divine sonship and a new creation. Those **"who are led by the Spirit . . . are not under the law"** (5.18).

The letter to the Galatians is included in the Church's liturgical lectionary, with the famous lines from the fourth chapter being the epistle reading of the Orthodox Church at the divine liturgy of Christmas (4.4–7). This letter also provides the Church with the verse which is sung at the solemn procession of the liturgy of baptism and chrismation, and which also replaces the Thrice-Holy Hymn at the divine liturgies of the great feasts of the Church which were once celebrations of the entrance of the catechumens into the sacramental life of the Church (see *Worship*, "Baptism").

> *For as many as have been baptized into Christ have put on Christ* (Gal 3.27).

EPHESIANS

The letters of St Paul to the Ephesians, Philippians and Colossians are called the captivity epistles since they are held to have been written by the apostle from his house arrest in Rome around 60 A.D. In some early sources, the letter to the Ephesians does not contain the words "who are at Ephesus," thus leading some to think of the epistle as a general letter meant for all of the churches.

St Paul's purpose in the letter to the Ephesians is to share his **"insight into the mystery of Christ"** (3.4) and **"to make all men see what is the plan of the for ages in God Who created all things . . ."** (3.9) In the first part of the letter, the apostle attempts to describe the mystery. He uses many words in long sentences, overflowing with adjectives, in his effort to accomplish his task. Defying a neat outline, the main points of the message are clear.

The plan of God for Christ, before the foundation of the world, is **"to unite all things in Him, things in heaven and things on earth"** (1.10) The plan is accomplished through the crucifixion, resurrection and glorification of Christ at the right hand of God. The fruits of God's plan are given freely to all men by God's free gift of grace, to Jews and gentiles alike, who believe-in the Lord. They are given in the One Holy Spirit, in the One Church of Christ, **"which is His body, the fullness of Him who fills all in all"** (1.23). In the Church of Christ, with each part of the body knit together and functioning properly in harmony and unity, man grows up in truth and in love "to the measure of the stature of the fullness of Christ" (4.12–16). He gains access to God the Father through Christ in the Spirit thus becoming **"a holy temple of the Lord . . . a dwelling place of God"** (2.18–22), **"filled with all the fullness, of God"** (3.19).

In the second part of the letter, St Paul spells out the implications of the **"great mystery . . . Christ and the Church"** (5.32). He urges sound doctrine and love, a true conversion of life, a complete end to all impurity and immorality and a total commitment to spiritual battle. He addresses the Church as a whole; husbands and wives, parents and children, masters and slaves. He calls all to "**put on the new nature, created after the likeness of God in true righteousness and holiness**" (4.24).

The letter to the Ephesians finds its place in the liturgical lectionary of the Church, with the well-known lines from the sixth chapter being the epistle reading at the sacramental celebration of marriage (5.21–33).

PHILLIPPIANS

As we have mentioned, the letter of St Paul to the Philippians was written at the time of his confinement in Rome. It is a most intimate letter of the apostle to those whom he sincerely loved in the Lord, those who were his faithful partners in the gospel "**from the first day until now**" (1.5). In this letter, St Paul exposes the most personal feelings of his mind and heart as he sees the approaching end of his life. He also praises the Philippian Church as a model Christian community in every way, encouraging and inspiring its beloved members whom he calls his "**joy and crown**" (4.1) with prayers that their "love may abound more and more with knowledge and all discernment," so that they "**may approve what is excellent, and may be pure and blameless for the day of Christ, filled with all the fruits of righteousness which come through Jesus Christ for the praise and glory of God**" (1.10–11).

Of special significance in the letter to the Philippians, besides the mention of "**bishops and deacons**" (1.1), which hints at the developing structure of the Church, is St Paul's famous passage about the self-emptying (**kenosis**) of Christ which is the epistle reading for the feasts of the Nativity and and Dormition of the Theotokos in the Orthodox Church, and which has been so influential for Christian spiritual life, particularly in Russia.

Have this mind among yourselves, which you have in Christ Jesus, who, though He was in the form of God, did not count equality with God a thing to be grasped, but emptied Himself, taking on the form of a servant (slave), and being born in the likeness of men. And being found in human form He humbled Himself and became obedient unto death, even death on a cross. Therefore God has highly exalted Him and bestowed on Him the name which is above every name . . . (2.5–9).

Like all Pauline epistles, the letter to Phillipians has its place in the Church's normal lectionary.

COLOSSIANS

It is believed that the letter of St Paul to the Colossians, written, as we have said, from Rome, was expressly intended to instruct the faithful in Colossae in the true Christian gospel in the face of certain heretical teachings which were threatening the community there. It appears that some form of gnosticism and angel worship had crept into the Colossian Church.

Gnosticism was an early Christian heresy which, in all of its various forms, denied the goodness of material, bodily reality, and therefore, the genuine incarnation, crucifixion and resurrection of Christ in human flesh. It made of the Christian faith a type of dualistic, spiritualistic philosophy which pretended to provide a secret knowledge of the divine by way of intellectual mysticism. **Gnosis**, as a word, means knowledge.

In his letter, St Paul stresses that he indeed wishes the Colossians to be **"filled with the knowledge of God's will in all spiritual wisdom and understanding"** (1.9), and that indeed it is true that in Christ **"are hid all the treasures of wisdom and knowledge"** (2.3). The real point of the Christian gospel, however, is that in Christ, through whom and for whom all things were created (1.16), **"the whole fulness of** deity dwells bodily" (2.9). It is only through the incarnation of Christ and His death on the cross and His resurrection from the dead, in the most real way, that salvation is given to men. It is given in the Church, through baptism; the Church which is itself Christ's **"body"** (1.24, 2.19).

Thus, the apostle insists to the Colossians that Christ is superior to all angels, having **"disarmed the principalities and powers** (i.e., the angels)... **triumphing over them"** on the cross" (2.15). He warns them, therefore **"to see to it that no one makes a prey of you by philosophy and vain deceit, according to human traditions, according to the elemental spirits of the uni-verse and not according to Christ"** (2.8). He warns as well that they should **"let no one disqualify you, insisting on self-abasement and worship of angels, taking his stand on visions, puffed up without reason by his sensuous mind . . ."** (2.18)

The content and style of the letter to the Colossians is very similar to **Ephesians.** Following the doctrinal instructions of the letter, their spiritual implications for the believer are spelled out with moral exhortations for a life lived in conformity to Christ and in total service to Him. Like the other letters of St Paul, the letter to Colossians is read in its turn in the liturgical services of the Church.

THESSALONIANS

It is generally agreed that St Paul's two letters to the Thessalonians are the first of the apostle's epistles, and are also the earliest written documents of the New Testament scriptures. They were most likely sent from Corinth, at the end of the forties, in response to the report brought from Timothy that certain difficulties had arisen in the Thessalonian Church about the second coming of Christ and the resurrection of the dead.

In both of his letters to the Thessalonians, St Paul repeats the same doctrine. He urges patient steadfastness of faith and continual love and service to the Lord and the brethren in the face of the many persecutions and trials which were confronting the faithful. He affirms that the Lord will come **"like a thief in the night"** (1 Thess 5.2) when all satanic attacks against the faith have been completed. But in the meantime, the Christians must continue **"to do their work in quietness"** (2 Thess 3.12) without panic or fear, and without laziness or idleness into which some had fallen because of their belief in the Lord's immediate return.

Concerning the resurrection from the dead, the apostle teaches that as Jesus truly rose, so will all **"those who have fallen asleep"** (Thess 4.14).

> For the Lord Himself will descend from heaven . . . and the dead in Christ will rise first; then we who are alive, who are left, shall be caught up together with them in the clouds to meet the Lord (1 Thess. 4.16–17).

This entire passage (1 Thess 4.16–17) is the epistle reading at the funeral liturgy in the Orthodox Church. Both letters to the Thessalonians are included in the liturgical lectionary during the Church year.

TIMOTHY

The letters of St Paul to Timothy and Titus are called the **pastoral epistles**. Although some modern scholars consider these letters as documents of the early second century, primarily because of the developed picture of Church structure which they present, Orthodox Church Tradition defends the letters as authentic epistles of St Paul from his house arrest in Rome in the early sixties of the first century.

The two letters to Timothy are of similar contents, having the same purpose to teach **"how one ought to behave in the household of God, which is the church of the living God, the pillar and bulwark of the truth"** (1 Tim 3.15).

In his first letter to Timothy, St Paul urges his **"true child in the faith"** (1.2), who was in Ephesus, to **"wage the good warfare, holding faith and a good conscience"** (1.18–19). He urges that prayers **"be made for all men"** by the Church (2.1) and that **"good doctrine"** be preserved and propagated, most particularly in times of difficulties and defections from the true faith (4.6, 6.3). In the letter, the apostle counsels all in proper Christian belief and behavior, giving special advice, both professional and personal, to his co-worker Timothy whom he counsels not to neglect the gift which he received **"when the elders laid their hands"** upon him (4.14).

The main body of the first letter to Timothy describes in detail the requirements for the pastoral offices of **bishop, deacon** and **presbyter** (priest or elder), and offers special instructions concerning the widows and slaves. The rules concerning the pastoral ministries have remained in the Orthodox Church, being formally incorporated into its canonical regulations.

Of special note in the first letter to Timothy is St Paul's confession of sinfulness which has become part of the pre-communion prayers of the Orthodox Church.

> *The saying is sure and worthy of full acceptance, that Christ Jesus came into the world to save sinners, of whom I am first* (1 Tim 1.15).

In his **second letter to Timothy,** St Paul again urges his **"beloved child"** to **"rekindle the gift of God that is within you through the laying on of my hands"** (1.2, 6). He stresses the absolute necessity for **"sound doctrine"** in the Church, calling for a firm struggle against **"godless chatter"** and the **"disputing over words"** (2.14,16) particularly in **"times of stress"** when the gospel is attacked by men of **"corrupt mind and counterfeit faith"** who are merely **"holding the form of religion but denying the power of it"** (3.1–8). As in his first letter, the apostle specifically mentions the need for the firm adherence to the scriptures (3.15).

The expression of St Paul in this letter, that the leaders of the Church must be found **"rightly handling the word of truth"** (2.15), has become the formal liturgical prayer of the Orthodox Church for its bishops.

TITUS

St Paul's letter to Titus in Crete is a shorter version of his two letters to Timothy. The author outlines the moral requirements of the **bishop** in the Church and urges the pastor always to **"teach what befits sound doctrine"** (1.9, 2.1). It tells how both the leaders and the faithful members of the Church should behave.

Sections of the letter to Titus about the appearance of **"the grace of God . . . for the salvation of all men . . . by the washing of regeneration and renewal in the Holy Spirit which He poured out upon us richly through Jesus Christ our Savior"** (2.11–3.7) comprise the Church's epistle reading for the feast of the Epiphany.

Generally speaking, each of the pastoral epistles is included in the Church's continual epistle lectionary, coming in the Church year just before the beginning of Great Lent.

PHILEMON

In his letter to Philemon written from his Roman imprisonment, St Paul appeals to his **"beloved fellow worker"** (1.1) to receive back his runaway slave Onesimus who had become a Christian, **"no longer as a slave, but as a beloved brother . . . both in the flesh and in the Lord."** (16) He asks Philemon to **"receive him as you would receive me"** (17) and offers to pay whatever debts Onesimus may have towards his master.

HEBREWS

Virtually none of the modern scriptural scholars think that St Paul is the author of the letter to the Hebrews. The question of the exact authorship of this epistle was questioned early in Church Tradition with the general consensus being that the inspiration and doctrine of the letter is certainly St Paul's, but that perhaps the actual writer of the letter was one of St Paul's disciples. The letter is dated in the second half of the first century and is usually read in the Church as being "of the holy apostle Paul."

The letter to the Hebrews begins with the clear teaching about the divinity of Christ, affirming that God, Who **"in many and various ways . . . spoke of old to our fathers"** has **"in these last days . . . spoken to us by a Son, Whom He appointed the heir of all things, through Whom He also created the world"** (1.1–2).

> *He (the Son of God) reflects the glory of God and bears the very stamp of His nature (or person), upholding the universe by the word of His power"* (1.3).

Christ, the divine Son of God, was made man as the **"apostle and high priest of our confession"** (3.1), **"the great shepherd of the sheep"** (13: 20), **"the pioneer and perfecter of our faith"** (12.2), whom God sent to **"taste of death for everyone"** (2.9).

> *He Himself . . . partook of the same nature (of human flesh and blood), that through death He might destroy him who has the power of death, that.is, the devil, and deliver all those who through fear of death were subject to lifelong bondage . . . (being) made like His brethren in every respect, so that He might become a merciful and faithful highpriest in the service of God, to make expiation for the sins of the people. For since He Himself has suffered and been tempted, He is able to help those who are tempted* (2.14–18).

The main theme of the letter to the Hebrews is to compare the sacrifice of Christ to the sacrifices of the priests of the Old Testament. The Old Testament priests made continual sacrifices of animals for themselves and the sins of the people, entering into the sanctuary of the Jerusalem temple. Christ makes the perfect and eternal sacrifice of Himself upon the cross, once and for all, for the sins of the people and not for Himself, entering into the heavenly sanctuary, not made by hands, **"to appear in the presence of God on our behalf"** (9.24). This is the perfect and all fulfilling sacrifice of the one perfect high priest of God Who was prefigured in the mysterious person of Melchizedek, in the Old Testament, as well as in the ritual priesthood of the Levites under the old law which was **"but a shadow of the good things to come"** and not yet the "true form of these realities" (10.1, See Gen 14, Ex 29, Lev 16, Ps 110).

Through the perfect sacrifice of Christ, the believers receive forgiveness of sins and are **"made perfect"** (11.40), being led and disciplined by God Himself Who gives His Holy Spirit that through their sufferings in imitation of Christ, His people **"may share in His holiness"** (12.10). This is effected, once again, not by the ritual works of the law which **"made nothing perfect"** (7.19), but by faith in God, without which **"it is impossible to please Him"** (11.6).

The letter to the Hebrews, which is read in the Orthodox Church at the divine liturgies during Great Lent, ends with the author's appeal to all to **"be grateful for receiving a kingdom which cannot be shaken"** and to **"offer to God acceptable worship with reverence and awe; for our God is a consuming fire"** (12.28). It calls as well for love, faith, purity, generosity, strength, obedience and joy among all who believe in **"Jesus Christ (Who) is the same yesterday and today and for ever"** (13.8).

Letters of St James

According to Church Tradition, the letter of James was written not by either of the apostles, but by the "brother of the Lord" who was the first bishop of the Church in Jerusalem (see Acts 15, Gal 1.19). The letter is addressed to the "twelve tribes in the dispersion" which most probably means the Christians not of the Jerusalem Church.

The main purpose of the letter of James is to urge Christians to be steadfast in faith and to do those works which are called for by the "perfect law" of Christ which is the "law of liberty" (1.25, 2.12). It aims to correct the false opinion that because Christians are freed from the ritual works of the Mosaic law through faith in Christ, they need not do any good works whatsoever and are not subject to any law at all. Thus, the author writes very clearly against the doctrine of salvation by "faith alone" without the good works that the believer must necessarily perform if his faith is genuine.

What does it profit, my brethren, if a man says he has faith but has not works. Can his faith save him? If a brother or sister is ill-clad and in lack of daily food and one of you says to them, "Go in peace, be warmed and filled," without giving them the things needed for the body, what does it profit? So faith by itself, if it has no works, is dead.

Show me your faith apart from your works, and I by my works will show you my faith. You believe that God is one; you do well. Even the demons believe—and shudder. Was not Abraham our father justified by works, when he offered his son Isaac upon the altar? You see that faith was active along with his works, and faith was completed by works, and the scripture was fulfilled which says, "Abraham believed God, and it was reckoned to him as righteousness;" and he was called the friend of God. You see that a man is justified by works and not by faith alone (2.14–24).

First among the good works which the letter insists upon most vehemently is the work of honoring and serving the poor and lowly without partiality and selfish greed which is the cause of all wars and injustices among men (2.1–7). The author is passionately opposed to any "friendship with the world" which makes man an "enemy of God" because of covetousness (4.1–4). He calls the rich to "weep and howl for the miseries which are coming" to them because of the "luxuries and pleasures" which they have attained at the expense of others whom they have exploited (5.1–6).

Together with his despising of wealth, James teaches the absolute necessity of "bridling the tongue," the "little member" which is a "fire" that man uses to boast, slander, condemn, swear, lie and speak evil against his brethren, "staining the whole body" and "setting aflame the whole cycle of nature" (3.1–12).

> *If anyone thinks he is religious, and does not bridle his tongue but deceives his heart, this man's religion is in vain. Religion that is pure and undefiled before God and the Father is this: to visit orphans and widows in their affliction, and to keep oneself unstained from the world* (1.26–27).

The teaching of the letter of James that "every good gift and perfect gift is from above coming down from the Father of lights" (1.17) has become part of the dismissal prayer of the divine liturgies of the Orthodox Church. The letter of James also provides the Church with the first epistle reading for its sacrament of the unction of the sick.

> *Is any among you suffering? Let him pray. Is any cheerful? Let him sing praise. Is any among you sick? Let him call for the presbyters (elders) of the Church, and let them pray over him, anointing him with oil in the name of the Lord; and the prayer of faith will save the sick man, and the Lord will raise him up; and if he has committed sins, he will*

be forgiven. Therefore confess your sins to one another, and pray for one another, that you may be healed (5.13–16).

Letters of St Peter

Most modern scholars do not think that St Peter actually wrote the two letters called by his name. They consider the first letter as coming from the end of the first century and the second letter from the first half of the second century. The Tradition of the Church, however, maintains the testimony of the letters themselves, ascribing them to the foremost leader of Christ's apostles writing from "Babylon," which was the early Church's name for Rome, on the eve of his martyrdom there in the latter half of the first century (see 1 Pet 5.13, 2 Pet 1.14).

The **first letter of St Peter** is a passionate plea to all of "God's People" to be strong in their sufferings in imitation of Christ and together with Him, maintaining "good conduct among the Gentiles," subjecting themselves without malice or vindictiveness to "every human institution for the Lord's sake" (2.11–13).

Special instructions and exhortations to godliness are addressed first to the whole Church which is a "chosen race, a royal priesthood, a holy nation, God's own people" (2.9), and then in turn to the slaves (2.18), to the husbands and wives (3.1–7) and to the presbyters [elders] whom the author, as a "fellow presbyter and a witness of the sufferings of Christ," calls to "tend the flock of God . . . not by constraint, but willingly, not for shameful gain, but eagerly, not as domineering over those in [their] charge, but being examples to the flock" (5.1–4).

Throughout the letter, the analogy is constantly drawn between the sufferings of Christ and the sufferings of Christians which is for their salvation.

But if when you do right and suffer for it you take it patiently, you have God's approval. For to this you have been called, because Christ suffered for you, leaving you an example, that you should follow in His steps. He committed no sin; no guile was found on His lips. When He was reviled, He did not revile in return; when He suffered, He did not threaten; but He trusted to Him Who judges justly. He Himself bore our sins in His body on the tree, that we might die to sin and live to righteousness. By His wounds you have been healed. For you were straying like sheep, but have now returned to the Shepherd and Guardian [literally Bishop] of your souls (2.20–25).

The **second letter of St Peter** is sometimes considered to be a sermon addressed to those who were newly baptized into the Christian faith. The author wishes before his death to "arouse . . . by way of reminder" (1.13, 3.1) what God has done for those who are called, that they might "escape from the corruption that is in the world through passion, and become partakers of the divine nature" (1.3–4). He warns against the appearance of "false prophets" and "scoffers" who would lead the elect astray by their "destructive heresies" and denials of "the Master who bought them" thus causing them to fall back to a life of sin and ignorance as "the dog turns back to his own vomit and the sow is washed only to wallow once more in the mire" (2.1–22, 3.1–7). The author makes special warning against the perversion of the holy scriptures, both those of the Old Testament and those of St Paul, "which the ignorant and unstable twist to their own destruction" (3.16, 1.20).

The third chapter of the second letter of St Peter is sometimes wrongly interpreted as teaching the total destruction of creation by God at the end of the world. The Orthodox interpretation is that it is only sin and evil that will be "dissolved with fire" on the "day of God," and that the "new heavens and a new earth in which righteousness dwells" wilt be the same "very good" world of God's original creation, but purified, renewed and purged of all that is contrary to His divine goodness and holiness (3.8–13).

The reminiscence in the second letter of St Peter about the trans-figuration of Christ is the epistle reading at the Church's feast of this sacred event (1.16–18). Readings from both letters are found in the Church's lectionary, with selections from the first letter being read at the vigil of the feast of Saints Peter and Paul.

Letters of St John

The three letters of St John were written by the Lord's beloved apostle who also wrote the fourth gospel. They were written at the close of the first century and have as their general theme a fervent polemic against the heretical "antichrists" who were changing the doctrines of Christ and denying His genuine appearance "in the flesh" for the salvation of the world, denying thereby both "the Father and the Son" (1 Jn 2.22, 4.3, 2 Jn 7).

The **first letter of St John** is the simplest and deepest exposition of the Christian faith that exists. Its clarity concerning the Holy Trinity and the Christian life of truth and of love in communion with God makes it understandable without difficulty to anyone who reads it. It is the best place to begin a study of the Christian faith generally, and the Bible in particular. The first letter begins in the same way as St John's gospel to which it is most similar in its entire content and style.

> *That which was from the beginning, which we have heard, which we have seen with our eyes, which we have looked upon and touched with our hands, concerning the Word of Life . . . we proclaim also to you, so that you may have communion with us; and our communion is with the Father and with His Son Jesus Christ. And we are writing this that our joy may be complete* (1.1–14).

The first letter of St John proclaims that Jesus is truly "the Christ," the Messiah and Son of God who has come "in the flesh" to the world as "the expiation of our sins, and not ours only, but also for the sins of the whole world" (2.2). Those who believe in Christ and are in communion with Him and His Father have the forgiveness of sins and the possibility not to sin any more (1.5–2.12). They "walk in the same way in which He walked" (2.6) being the "children of God" (3.1, 5.1). They know the truth by the direct inspiration of God through the anointment [chrisma] of the Holy Spirit (2.20–26; 6.7). They keep the commandments of God, the first and greatest of which is love, and so they are already recipients of eternal life, already possessing the indwelling of God the Father and Christ the Son "by the Spirit which He has given us" (2.24–3.24).

> *Beloved, let us love one another; for love is of God, and he who loves is born of God and knows God. He who does not love does not know God; for God is love. In this the love of God was made manifest among us, that God has sent His only Son into the world, so that we might live through Him.*
>
> *In this is love, not that we loved God but that He loved us and sent His Son to be the expiation of our sins. Beloved, if God so loved us, we also ought to love one another. No man has ever seen God; if we love one another, God abides in us and His love is perfected in us.*
>
> *By this we know that we abide in Him and He in us, because He has given us of His own Spirit. And we have seen and testify that the Father has sent His Son as the Savior of the world. Whoever confesses that Jesus is the Son of God, God abides in him and he in God. So we know and believe the love God has for us. God is love, and he who abides in love abides in God, and God abides in him* (14.7–16).

The hatred of others is the sure sign that one does not love God (4.20) and is "in the darkness still" (2.9–11). The one who hates his brother is "a murderer, and you know that no murderer has eternal life abiding in him" (3.15). Those who love God are hated by the world which is in the power of the evil one" (5.19, 2.15–17).

The first letter of St John is part of the Church's lectionary, with special selections from it being read at the feast of the apostle John.

The **second letter of St John** is addressed to the "elect lady and her children" which is obviously the Church of God and its members. Again the truth of Christ is stressed and the commandment of love is emphasized.

> *And this is love, that we follow His commandments; this is the commandment, as you have heard from the beginning, that you follow love. For many deceivers have gone out into the world, men who will not acknowledge the coming of Jesus Christ in the flesh; such a one is the deceiver and the antichrist. Look to yourselves, that you may not lose what you have worked for, but may win a full reward. Anyone who goes ahead and does not abide in the doctrine of Christ does not have God; he who abides in the doctrine has both the Father and the Son (6–9).*

The **third letter of St John** is addressed to a certain Gaius praising him for the "truth of his life" (3) and urging him not to Imitate evil but imitate good" (11). "No greater joy can I have than this", writes the beloved apostle, "to hear that my children follow the truth" (4).

Letter of St Jude

It has been questioned whether "Jude, the servant of Jesus Christ and the brother of James" who wrote the letter of St Jude is the "Judas, the brother of James" (Lk 6.16, Acts 1.13), one of the twelve apostles, "not Iscariot" (Jn 14.22). In the Tradition of the Church, the two have usually been identified as the same person.

The letter of St Jude is a general epistle which the author "found it necessary to write to those who are called," appealing to them "to contend for the faith which was once for all delivered to the saints" (1–3).

For admission has been secretly gained by some who long ago were designated for condemnation, ungodly persons who pervert the grace of our God into licentiousness and deny our only Master and Lord Jesus Christ (4).

These "scoffers," some of whom the faithful may be able to save "by snatching them out of the fire" (23), are those who "defile the flesh, reject authority and revile the glorious ones" (8). They are those who follow their "ungodly passions ... [and] set up divisions, worldly people devoid of the Spirit" (18–19) who have entered the Church,

Jude commands those who are faithful to resist the ungodly.

But you, beloved, build yourselves up on your holy faith; pray in the Holy Spirit; keep yourselves in the love of God; wait for the mercy of our Lord Jesus Christ unto eternal life. . . . (21).

Of special interest in the letter, which is sometimes read in Church, is the mention of the archangel Michael (9), as well as the evil angels "that did not keep their own position but left their proper dwelling (with God) and have been kept by Him in eternal chains in the nether gloom until the judgment of the great day" (6). Generally speaking, there is a definite apocalyptic tone to the letter of St Jude.

Book of Revelation

The **Book of Revelation**, also called the **Apocalypse** which means that which has been disclosed, and also called the **Revelation to St John**, is traditionally considered to be the work of the Lord's apostle who later wrote the fourth gospel and the letters. It is dated in the middle of the last half of the first century.

St John received his vision "on the island called Patmos." He was "in the Spirit on the Lord's day" when he received God's command to write the letters "to the seven churches of Asia" (1.4–10). Each of the seven messages contains the words of Christ for the specific church (2–4).

Following the seven letters in the book of **Revelation**, the apostle records his vision of God on His throne in heaven being hymned unceasingly by angels, the "living creatures", and the "twenty four elders": "Holy, holy, holy, is the Lord God Almighty, Who was and is and is to come" (4).

There then follows the prophecies of the seven seals and the seven angels (5–11), and the visions of the "women clothed with the sun" and Michael and his angels engaged in battle with the "dragon" (12). Next come the images of the "beast rising from the sea" and the "other beast rising from the earth" (13). Then comes the vision of the Lamb and those who are saved by God, with the angels coming to earth from heaven bearing their "bowls of wrath" (14–16). The image of the "great harlot" follows (17), with the final prophecy about the downfall of "great Babylon" (18). The end of the book of Revelation describes the wonderful vision of salvation, with the multitude of those "blessed . . . who are invited to the marriage supper of the Lamb" in the midst of the great celestial assembly of angels who sing glory to God and to Jesus, His word and His Lamb, the Alpha and the Omega, the King of kings and the Lord of lords. It is the image of the Kingdom of God and of Christ, the Heavenly Jerusalem foretold by the prophets of old in which the righteous shall reign forever with God (19–22).

> *Hallelujah! For the Lord our God the Almighty reigns. Let us rejoice and exalt and give Him the glory, for the marriage of the Lamb has come, and the Bride (the Church) has made herself ready. . . .* (19.6–7).

> *Then I saw a new heaven and a new earth; for the first heaven and the first earth had passed away. . . . And I saw the holy city, new Jerusalem, coming down from heaven from God, prepared as a bride adorned for her husband; and I heard a great voice from the throne*

saying, "Behold, the dwelling of God is with men. He will dwell with them and they shall be His People, and God Himself will be with them; He will wipe away every tear from their eyes, and death shall be no more, neither shall there be mourning nor crying nor pain anymore, for the former things have passed away" (21.1–4).

And He Who sat upon the throne said, "Behold, I make all things new" (21.5).

It is done! I am the Alpha and the Omega, the Beginning and the End. To the thirsty I will give water without price from the fountain of life. He who conquers shall have this inheritance, and I will be his God and he shall be My son (21.6–7).

There was a certain hesitation on the part of the early Church to include the book of Revelation in the canonical scriptures of the New Testament. The reason for this was obviously the great difficulty of interpreting the apocalyptic symbols of the book. Nevertheless, since the document carried the name of the apostle John, and since it was inspired by the Holy Spirit for the instruction and edification of the Church, it came to be the last book listed in the Bible, although it is never read liturgically in the Orthodox Church.

It is indeed difficult to interpret the book of Revelation, especially if one is unfamiliar with the images and symbols of the apocalyptic writings of the Bible, that is the Old Testament, and of the Judeo-Christian Tradition. There exists, however, a traditional approach to the interpretation of the book within the Church which offers insight into its meaning for the faithful.

The wrong method of interpreting the book of Revelation is to give some sort of exclusive meaning to its many visions, equating them with specific, concrete historical events and persons, and to fail to understand the symbolical significance of the many images which are used by the author following biblical and traditional sources.

First of all, the letters to the seven churches have both a historical and a universal meaning. The messages are clear and remain relevant to situations which have always existed in the Church and which exist today. For example, many older churches in all ages of history can be identified with the Church of Ephesus. Those under persecution can be compared with the Church in Smyrna. And not a few—perhaps some in America right now—can be judged with the Church in Laodicea. The seven letters remain forever as "prototypical" of churches that will exist until Christ's kingdom comes.

The visions and prophecies of the main body of the book of Revelation present great difficulties, but mostly to those interpreters who would attempt to apply them to one or another historical event or person. If the general vision and prophecy of the book is seen as revealing the correlation between events "in heaven" and events "on earth," between God and man, between the powers of goodness and the powers of evil, then, though many difficulties obviously remain, some will also immediately disappear.

In the book of Revelation, one comes to understand that the Kingdom of God is always over all and before all. One sees as well that the battle between the righteous and the evil is perpetually being waged. There are always the faithful who belong to the Lamb, being crowned and robed by Him for their victories. There are always the "beasts" and the "dragons" which need to be defeated. The "great harlot" and the "great Babylon" are forever to be destroyed. The "heavenly Jerusalem" is perpetually coming, and one day it will come and the final victory will be complete.

One notices as well that there is a universality and finality about the symbols and images of the book of Revelation, a meaning to be applied to them which has already been revealed in the scriptures of the Old Testament. Thus, for example, the image of Babylon stands for every society which fights against God, every body of persons united in wickedness and fleshliness. The image of harlotry universally applies as well to all who are corrupted by their passions and lusts, unfaithful to God Who has made them and loves them. The symbolic numerology also remains constant, with the number 666 (13.18), for example, symbolizing total depravity, unlike 7 which is the symbol of fulness; and the number 144,000 (14.3) being the symbol of total completion and the full number of the saved, the result of the multiplication of 12 times 12—the number of the tribes of Israel and the apostles of Christ. Thus, through the images of the book of Revelation, a depth of penetration into universal spiritual realities is disclosed which is greater than any particular earthly reality. The insight into the meaning of the book depends on the inspiration of God and the purity of heart of those who have eyes to see and ears to hear and minds willing and able to understand.

In the Orthodox Church, the book of Revelation has great liturgical significance. The worship of the Church has traditionally, quite consciously, been patterned after the divine and eternal realities revealed in this book. The prayer of the Church and its mystical celebration are one with the prayer and celebration of the kingdom of heaven. Thus, in Church, with the angels and saints, through Christ the Word and the Lamb, inspired by the Holy Spirit, the faithful believers of the assembly of the saved offer perpetual adoration to God the Father Almighty.

The book of Revelation, although never read in the Orthodox Church, bears witness to the divine reality which is the Church's own very life.

> *The Spirit and the Bride [the Church] say, "Come." And let him who hears say, "Come." And let him who is thirsty come, let him who desires take the water of life without price.*
> *"Surely I am coming soon" [says Jesus, the Lord].*
> *Amen. Come, Lord Jesus!* (22.17, 20)

7

SALVATION
HISTORY

Word and Spirit

It is the constant testimony of the Bible and the Church that God acts toward the world through **His Word** and **His Spirit.**

God created all things by His Word and His Spirit. He created man in His divine image and likeness to partake of His Word and to live by His Spirit. All of the holy people of God received the Word of God and the Spirit of God. The patriarchs, prophets, and apostles all proclaimed the Word which came to them from God by the Spirit of God. The law of Moses and the prophets, the psalms and all the scriptures of the Old and New Testaments are the Word of God, written and interpreted by men through the Spirit of God. Always and everywhere in the Bible and in the Church, God reveals Himself and acts in man and the world by His Word and His Spirit.

The central affirmation of the Christian Faith and the very essence of its gospel and life is that the Word of God became man as Jesus of Nazareth, the Messiah of Israel and the Lord and Savior of the world. Jesus of Nazareth is the divine Word of God in human form. He is the personal Word of God Who was "in the beginning with God," the Word "by whom all things were made" (Jn 1.2). He is the uncreated Word of God according to Whose image all men are created. He is the Word of God Who came to the patriarchs and prophets and Who is incarnate in the Bible in scriptural form. He is the Word of God Who died on the cross and is risen from the dead. He is the Head of the Church which is His Body, and the King of the Kingdom of God. He is the Word of God with Whom and through Whom the Holy Spirit comes to the world.

The Holy Spirit of God comes personally to men from the Father through Jesus Christ, the incarnate Word of God. He comes to those who believe in Christ and belong to Him through faith and repentance and baptism in His Church. He is the Spirit Who descended upon the disciples on Pentecost, who also is the Ont by whose power the world was created and continued to exist. He is the Spirit breathed into men by God to make them live according to His divine likeness. He is the Spirit Who inspired the Law, and the prophets and the entire holy scripture, providing for its production and preservation, as well as for its interpretation ir the life of the faithful. He is the same Holy Spirit Who abides in the Church, making possible the fulness of its sacramental and spiritual life. He is the Spirit of God Who, by His presence with men in the world, is the pledge and the promise of God's Kingdom to come. He is the Holy Spirit of God Who will one day, on the Day of the Lord, fill all creation with the presence of God.

Thus, the entire creation, the salvation and glorification of the world, the whole of what we call "salvation history," depends on God and His Word and His Spirit, the Most Holy Trinity, Who in the Church and in the Kingdom, "fills all in all" (Eph 1.23).

Pre-History

The Bible begins with the story of creation and the making of man. Although the Bible often lists the generations of men from the creation of Adam (Chron 1.1, Lk 4.38), the history of salvation, in the most proper sense, begins with Abraham, the forefather of Israel and the first ancestor of Christ, "according to the flesh."

The story of creation, and specifically of Adam and Eve, gives the divine revelation about the absolute sovereignty of God over all of creation. It tells of the goodness of all things that exist, and the superiority of man over other beings. It shows how the origin of evil does not lie in God but in His most perfect creature whose free act of sin brought wickedness and death to the world.

The chapters of Genesis 1–11 are called the "prehistory" of salvation because with little exception, such as that of the righteous Noah, these chapters are almost exclusively the record of sin. They begin with man's original rebellion against God, and tell of the first act of man's children as being brotherly murder. They record God's sadness in creating the world when He "saw that the wickedness of man was great in the earth, and that every imagination of his heart was only evil continually," and that the earth was "corrupt . . . 'filled with violence . . . for all flesh had corrupted their way upon the earth" (Gen 6.5–12). They end with the symbolic account of the ultimate impudence of men who sought "to make a name for themselves" by building "a tower with its top in the heavens" (Gen 11.4). Through the story of the tower of Babel is shown the prideful arrogance of man which results in the division of the nations and the scattering of men "over the face of all the earth" (Gen 11.9).

The pre-history of salvation, the story of sin, is the original counter-symbol of salvation in Christ. The events of these first chapters of the Bible, before the calling of Abraham, find their proper interpretation in the saving events of the coming of Christ and the Holy Spirit in the new and final covenant of God with His People.

Christ is the True Adam. The original Adam was merely "a type of him who was to come" (Rom 5.14).

> For as in Adam all die, so also in Christ shall all be made alive.
>
> Thus it is written, "The first man Adam became a living soul;" the last Adam [Christ] became a life-giving spirit. But it is not the spiritual which is first but the physical, and then the spiritual. The first man was from the earth, a man of dust; the second man is from heaven. As was the man of dust, so are those who are of the dust; and as is the man of heaven, so are those who are of heaven. Just as we have borne the image of the man of dust, we shall also bear the image of the man of heaven (1 Cor 15.21–22, 45–49).

The word **Adam** in Hebrew comes from "adamah" which means earth. The word **Christ**, in Hebrew, **Messiah**, means the "anointed" of God. As Christ is the new Adam, so His mother Mary is the new Eve, for she is the true "mother of all living," which is the meaning of the name given to the original "helper" of man (Gen 3.20). The biblical symbolism continues with the Church of Christ being the true "ark of salvation" in which "every living thing" is saved (Gen 6.14, 1 Pet 3.20–22). And the events of Pentecost reverse the tragedy of Babel, when through the descent of the Holy Spirit upon the Church of Christ, all national divisions are overcome and all men "from over the face of all the earth" are brought into unity by God in Christ.

Thus the pre-history of man's sin is the counter-symbol of his righteousness in God which is realized in Christ, the "child of Abraham" in whose children all of the families of the earth are blessed by God (Gen 12.3).

Abraham

Salvation history, properly so-called, begins with Abram, whom God named **Abraham** which means "father of a multitude." Abraham was the first patriarch of the people of Israel. The word **patriarch** means "the father of the people." In the person and life of Abraham, the central events of the salvation of the world by Christ in the New Testament have been prefigured.

God made the first promise of His salvation of all the people of the earth to Abraham, with whom He also made His covenant to be faithful forever.

> *Now the Lord said to Abram, "Go from your country and kindred and your father's house to the land that I will show you. And I will make you a great nation, and make your name great, so that you will*

be a blessing . . . and in you all families of the earth shall be blessed" (Gen 12.1–3, See also 17.1–8, 22.1–18).

The fulfillment of the promise to Abraham comes in Jesus Christ. He is the descendent of Israel's first father in whom all the families of the earth are blessed. Thus, Mary, the Mother of Jesus, sings at her time of waiting for the Savior's birth, that all generations will call her blessed because the fulfillment has come from God "as He spoke to our fathers, to Abraham and to his posterity forever" (Lk 1.55, see also Zachariah's Song in Lk 1.67–79). All through the New Testament the claim is made that God's promise to Abraham is fulfilled in Jesus.

Now the promises were made to Abraham and to his offspring. It does not say, "And to off springs," referring to many; but, referring to one, "And to your offspring," which is Christ (Gal 3.16).

The faith of Abraham is prototypical of al those who in Christ are saved by faith. The New Testament stresses faith as necessary for salvation. The model for this faith is Abraham.

Abraham believed God, and it was reckoned to him as righteousness (Gen 15.6, Rom 4.3).

Abraham's faith was united to his works, and was expressed in his works.

Was not Abraham our father justified by works, when he offered his son Isaac upon the altar? You see that faith was active along with his works, and faith was completed by works, and the scripture was fulfilled which says, "Abraham believed God, and it was reckoned to him as righteousness;" and he was called the friend of God. You see that a man is justified by works and not by faith alone (Jas 2.21–24).

God tested Abraham by commanding him to sacrifice his beloved son Isaac as a burnt offering. Abraham believed and trusted in God.

He obeyed his will, and went to the mountain to slay his child. God stopped him and placed a ram in Isaac's place saying "for now I know that you fear God, seeing that you have not withheld your son, your only son, from me" (Gen 22.12). Then once more God made the promise that "by your descendants shall all of the nations of the earth be blessed . . ." (Gen 22.18).

The sacrifice of Isaac is not only a testimony to Abraham's faith. It is also the original sign that God Himself does what He does not allow the first and foremost of His People to do. No ram is put in the place of God's Son, His only Son Jesus, when He is sacrificed on the cross for the sins of the world.

The perfect **priesthood** of Christ is also prefigured in Abraham's life. It is the priesthood of Melchizedek, the King of Peace. It is the priesthood in which the offering is bread and wine. It is the priesthood which is before that of the Levites, and the one which is that of the Messiah, Who is "a priest forever according to the order of Melchizedek" (Ps 110.4, Heb 5–10).

> *So also Christ did not exalt Himself to be made a high priest, but was appointed by Him Who said to Him, "Thou art my Son, today I have begotten thee;" as He says also in another place, "Thou art a priest for ever, after the order of Melchizedek."*
>
> *In the days of His flesh, Jesus offered up prayers and supplications, with loud cries and tears, to Him Who was able to save Him from death, and He was heard for His godly fear. Although He was a Son, He learned obedience through what He suffered; and being made perfect He became the source of eternal*

*salvation to all who obey Him, being designated by God a high priest
after the order of Melchizedek* (Heb 5.5–10).

*For this Melchizedek, king of Salem, priest of the Most High God,
met Abraham returning from the slaughter of the kings and blessed
him; and to him Abraham apportioned a tenth part of everything.
He is first, by translation of his name, king of righteousness, and then
he is also king of Salem, that is king of peace. He is without father
or mother or genealogy, and has neither beginning of days nor end
of life, but resembling the Son of God he continues a priest for ever*
(Heb 7.1–3).

The most sublime of the New Testament revelations, that of
the **Holy Trinity**, was also prefigured in Abraham's life. This is the
famous visit of the three angels of God to Abraham under the oaks
of Mamre.

*And the Lord appeared to him by the oaks of Mamre, as he sat at
the door of his tent in the heat of the day. He lifted up his eyes and
looked, and behold, three men stood in front of him. When he saw
them, he ran from the tent door to meet them, and bowed himself to
the earth, and said, "My lord, if I have found favor in your sight, do
not pass by your servant. Let a little water be brought, and wash your
feet, and rest yourselves under the tree, while I fetch a morsel of bread,
that you may refresh yourselves, and after that you may pass on . . .
since you have come to your servant." So they said, "Do as you have
said"* (Gen 18.1–5).

Abraham addresses the three angels as one, calling them Lord.
They eat in his presence and foretell the birth of Isaac from Sarah in her
old age. In this visitation of God to Abraham, the Orthodox Church
sees the prefiguration of the full revelation of the Holy Trinity in the
New Testament.

Because there can be no depiction of God the Father and the Holy Spirit in human form, Orthodox iconography has traditionally painted the Holy Trinity in the form of the three angels who came to Abraham. The most famous icon of the Holy Trinity, the one often used in the Church on the feast of Pentecost, is that of Saint Andrew Rublev, a disciple of Saint Sergius of Radonezh in Russia in the fourteenth century.

Thus the salvation of the world which has come in Christ was prefigured in the life of Abraham, as well as the Christian doctrine about faith and works and the Christian revelations about the sacrifice, the priesthood, and even the most Holy Trinity. Truly in Abraham every aspect of the final covenant in Christ the Messiah was foreshadowed and foretold.

Passover

The central event of the entire Old Testament history is the **passover** and **exodus**.

Abraham's son Isaac was the father of Jacob whom God named Israel which means "**he who strives with God**" (Gen 32.28). God renewed His promise to **Isaac** and **Jacob**, and continued the covenant with them that He had made with Abraham.

Jacob had twelve sons who became the leaders of the twelve tribes or houses of Israel. The sons of Jacob sold their youngest brother **Joseph** into slavery in Egypt. With the help of God, Joseph gained the favor of the Egyptian pharaoh and became a great man in Egypt. In a time of famine, Joseph's brothers came to Egypt for food. Joseph recognized them and brought all of the people of Israel into Egypt with him. When Joseph died, the people of Israel were put into slavery by the Egyptians for four hundred years (See Gen 24–50).

God raised up **Moses** to lead His people out of bondage in Egypt. He appeared to Moses in the burning bush and revealed His Name to him.

> *Then Moses said to God, "If I come to the people of Israel and say to them, 'The God of your fathers has sent me to you,' and they ask me, 'What is his name?' what shall I say to them?"*
>
> *God said to Moses, "I AM WHO I AM." And He said, "Say to the people of Israel, 'I AM has sent me to you.'"*
>
> *God also said to Moses, "Say this to the people of Israel, 'The Lord (Yahweh), the God of your fathers, the God of Abraham, the God of Isaac, the God of Jacob, has sent me to you': this is my name for ever, and thus I am to be remembered throughout all generations"* (Ex 3.14–15).

Moses returned to Egypt and after many trials with the Egyptian pharaoh and after many plagues, which God sent upon the Egyptians, he led the people of Israel out of slavery. The **exodus**, which means the escape or the departure, from Egypt took place on the night called the **passover**.

God, through Moses, ordered the Israelites to select lambs, to kill them and place some blood on the two doorposts and the lintel of their houses. Standing up, clothed and ready to escape, they were to eat the lambs in the night.

> *In this manner you shall eat it: your loins girded, your sandals on your feet and your staff in your hand; and you shall eat in haste. It is the Lord's passover. For I will pass through the land of Egypt that night, and I will smite all the firstborn in the land of Egypt, both man and beast; and on all the gods of Egypt I will execute judgments: I am the Lord. The blood shall be a sign for you, upon the houses where you are; and when I see the blood, I will pass over you, and no plague shall fall upon you to destroy you, when I smite the land of Egypt. This*

day shall be a memorial day, and you shall keep it as a feast to the Lord; throughout your generations you shall observe it as an ordinance forever (Ex 12.11–13).

Thus, the passover and exodus took place. At midnight the Lord slew the Egyptian firstborn. The houses marked with blood were spared when the Lord passed over. During the tumult, the Israelites began to escape. They made their exodus through the Red Sea. By this time, the Egyptian horsemen were in pursuit. At the sea, Moses prayed to God. He lifted his rod over the waters and "**The Lord drove the sea back by a strong East wind all night, and made the sea dry land . . .** " (Ex 14.21) The Israelites passed through the sea on foot. The pursuing chariots of the Egyptians were caught in the waters and were drowned.

And Israel saw the great work, which the Lord did against the Egyptians, and the people feared the Lord; and they believed in the Lord and in His servant Moses (Ex 14.31).

In the wilderness on the other side of the sea, the people of Israel began to complain. There was no food and drink in the desert. Moses prayed to the Lord, Who provided water for the people to drink and manna, the "bread from heaven," for the people to eat (Ex 15–16). God led the people through the desert by a cloud and a pillar of fire.

On Mount Sinai, Moses received the Ten Commandments and the laws of morality and worship from the Lord Who "**used to speak to Moses face to face, as a man speaks to his friend**" (Ex 33.11). Moses was allowed to behold the glory of the Lord in the smoke and clouds on the mountaintop and he himself shone with the majesty of God (Ex 34.29).

Moses was not granted to cross the Jordan and to enter the promised land. He died and was buried near Mount Nebo in the land of

Moab. This is where he had looked across the Jordan River into the land where his successor Joshua would lead the people.

The passover and exodus was the central event in Israelite history. It was remembered in all generations as the great sign of God's fidelity and favor to His People. It was sung about in the psalms and recalled by the prophets. It was celebrated annually together with Pentecost, as the chief celebration of the People of God. And, consequently, it was also the main event of the Old Testament to be fulfilled perfectly and eternally in the time of Christ, the Messiah of God.

In Jesus Christ the ultimate meaning and universal purpose of the passover and exodus are revealed and accomplished. Jesus Christ is Himself the **New Passover**. He is the **Passover Lamb**, which is slain for the deliverance and liberation of all men and the whole world from the powers of evil. The real "pharaoh" is the devil. He holds all men in slavery. The real deliverer is Jesus. He leads the people from the captivity of sin and death into the "promised land" of the Kingdom of God.

As the people pass through the wilderness of life in this world, they are fed by Jesus, the true Bread of Life, the true "bread from heaven."

> *Jesus said to them, "Truly, truly I say to you, it was not Moses who gave you the bread from heaven; my Father gives you the true bread from heaven. For the bread of God is that which came down from heaven, and gives life to the world."*
>
> *"I am the bread of life; he who comes to me shall not hunger, and he who believes in me shall never thirst."*
>
> *"I am the bread of life. Your fathers ate the manna in the wilderness and they died. This is the bread, which comes down from heaven that a man may eat of it and not die. I am the living bread which came down from heaven; if any one eats of this meal, he will live forever; and the bread which I shall give for the life of the world is my flesh."*

"Truly, truly I say to you, unless you eat the flesh of the Son of Man and drink his blood, you have no life in you; he who eats my flesh and drinks my blood has eternal life, and I will raise him up at the last day. For my flesh is food indeed, and my blood is drink indeed. He who eats my flesh and drinks my blood abides in me and I in him. As the living Father has sent me, and I live because of the Father, so he who eats me will live because of me. This is the bread which came down from heaven, not such as the fathers ate and died; he who eats this bread will live forever" (Jn 6.25–59).

Jesus is not only the true "bread from heaven," He is also the true "**living water.**" He is the One Whom, if men drink of Him, they will never thirst again.

"If anyone is thirsty, let him come to me and drink. He who believes in me, as the scripture has said, 'Out of his heart shall flow rivers of living water.'" (Jn 7.37)

". . . whoever drinks of the Water that I shall give him will become in him a spring of water welling up to eternal life" (Jn 4.14).

Saint Paul, speaking of the exodus and the rock, which Moses struck, from which the spring of water flowed, says plainly that this refers to Christ.

I want you to know, brethren, that our fathers were all under the cloud, and all passed through the sea, and all were baptized into Moses in the cloud and in the sea, and all ate the same spiritual food and all drank the same spiritual drink. For they drank from the spiritual Rock which followed them, and the Rock was Christ. (1 Cor 10.1–4)

Thus it is that Jesus Christ fulfilled the passover and exodus in the events of His life. This fulfillment came to its climax at the time of His crucifixion and resurrection. Jesus was killed at the feast of the passover to show that the old passover has been completed and the new passover has begun. When the paschal lamb was being killed in the temple, Jesus, the **Lamb of God**, was being crucified on the cross outside the city. When the great day of the passover, which that year was the Sabbath, was being observed as the rest from work, Jesus lay dead, resting from all His work, in the tomb. When the "day after Sabbath" dawned, the first day of the week, the day of God's original creation, Jesus arose from the dead.

All of this took place that the New Passover and New Exodus could be effected, not from Egypt into Canaan, but from death to life, from wickedness to righteousness, from darkness to light, from earth to heaven, from the tyranny of the devil to the glorious freedom of the Kingdom of God. The death and resurrection of Christ is the true passover-exodus of the People of God. Those who are marked with Christ's blood are spared from the visitation of death.

Jesus inaugurated the celebration of the new passover at the **last supper** with His disciples, which was the paschal meal. He told them that no longer would they keep the passover feast in remembrance of the old exodus. They now would keep the paschal celebration in remembrance of Him.

> For I received from the Lord what I also delivered to you, that the Lord Jesus on the night when He was betrayed took bread, and when He had given thanks, He broke it, and said, "This is my body which is broken for you. Do this in remembrance of me." In the same way also the cup, after supper, saying, "This cup is the new covenant in my blood. Do this, as often as you drink it, in remembrance of me." For as often as you eat this bread and drink the cup, you proclaim the Lord's death until He comes (1 Cor 2.23–26; see also Mat 26.26–29, Mk 14.22–25, Lk 22.14–19).

In the same letter, Saint Paul also says:

. . . Christ our Passover Lamb has been sacrificed. Let us, therefore, celebrate the festival, not with the old leaven, the leaven of malice and evil, but with the unleavened bread of sincerity and truth (1 Cor 5.7–8).

Of great importance also in the new passover of Christ is the new gift of God's law, the law not written on tablets of stone, but on human hearts by the very **Holy Spirit of God** (See 2 Cor 3, Jer 31.31–34, Ezek 36.26–27, Joel 2.28–29).

The giving of the law to Moses on Mount Sinai is fulfilled in the time of the Messiah in the giving of the Holy Spirit to the Disciples of Christ in the upper room on the feast of Pentecost. In the Old Testament, this was the festival of the reception of the law, fifty days after the passover (Acts 2). Thus, once again, in the time of the Messiah, the old event is completed in the new and final one: the exterior law of Moses is completed by the interior law of Christ, the "**perfect law, the law of liberty**" (Jas 1.25, 2.12), the "**law of the Holy Spirit**" (Rom 8.2).

For the law of the Spirit of life in Christ Jesus has set me free from the law of sin and death. For God had done (in Christ) what the law (of Moses), weakened by the flesh, could not do: sending His own Son in the likeness of sinful flesh and for sin . . . in order that the just requirements of the law (of Moses) might be fulfilled in us, who walk not according to the flesh, but according to the Spirit (Rom 8.2–4, See also 2 Cor 3, Gal 3–5).

Thus the apostle John writes: "**For the law was given through Moses; grace and truth came through Jesus Christ**" (Jn 1.17).

Within the total fulfillment and perfection of the passover-exodus of the Old Testament in the time of the Messiah, it must be noted as well that the crossing of the Jordan into the promised land corresponds to baptism in Christ into the Kingdom of God. Also worthy of note is the symbolic fact that the one who actually crossed the Jordan and brought the people into the "**land flowing with milk and honey,**" was not Moses but **Joshua**, whose name in Greek is **Jesus**, thus prefiguring the One Who was to come of the same name, which means Savior, the One Who began His messianic mission of bringing the Kingdom of God by His baptism in the Jordan River.

Thus, every aspect of the old passover-exodus is completed in Christ, perfectly, totally and forever. All of this is renewed and relived in the Church of Christ each year on Easter and Pentecost, and on each Sunday, the Day of the Lord. Whenever the Church gathers, it celebrates the perfect passover of Christ the Lamb of God, Who is also the divine I AM Who exists eternally with God the Father and the Holy Spirit, Who was slain for the life of the world.

Kingship

In the Old Testament, God was to be the King of His People. But wishing to be like the other nations, the Israelites asked the Lord for a human king.

> *Then all the elders of Israel gathered together and came to Samuel at Ramah, and said to him, "Behold, you are old and your sons do not walk in your ways; now appoint for us a king to govern us like all the nations." But the thing displeased Samuel when they said, "Give us a king to govern us." And Samuel prayed to the Lord. And the Lord said to Samuel, "Hearken to the voice of the people in all that they say to you; for they have not rejected you, but they have rejected me from being king over them. According to all the deeds which they have done to me, from the day I brought them up out of Egypt even to this day, forsaking me and serving other gods, so they are also doing to you. Now then, hearken to their voice; only you shall solemnly warn them, and show them the ways of the king who shah reign over them"* (1 Sam 8.4–9).

So Samuel recounted to the people all that would happen to them if they lived like the other nations having a man as their king. The king would send their sons to war. He would put all the people to work for him. He would take their best animals and crops. He would make the people his slaves.

"And in that day you will cry out because of your king, whom you have chosen for yourselves; but the Lord will not answer you in that day." But the people refused to listen to the voice of Samuel; and they said, "No! but we will have a king over us, that we also may be like all the nations, and that our king may govern us and go out before us and fight our battles." And when Samuel had heard all the words of the people, he repeated them in the ears of the Lord. And the Lord said to Samuel, "Hearken to their voice, and make them a king" (1 Sam 8.18–22).

Israel received its king. The first was Saul who became demented. The second was David the Shepherd who ruled well. The third was Solomon who was known for his wisdom and who built the temple to God in Jerusalem. But then there was a division of the kingdoms of Israel and Judah, and strife among them because of their sins, which resulted in a succession of captivities to various foreign powers from which the people never finally escaped.

The psalms and prophets of the Old Testament constantly recalled God's people to the reality that only the Lord is king. He alone is the True Shepherd of His People. He alone is the One Who rules and Who is to be served and obeyed.

I will extol Thee, my God and King,
and bless Thy name for ever and ever.
Every day I will bless Thee,
and praise Thy name for ever and ever.
Great is the Lord, and greatly to be praised,
and His greatness is unsearchable,

All Thy works shall give thanks to Thee, O Lord,
and all Thy saints shall bless Thee!
They shall speak of the glory of Thy kingdom and tell of Thy power,
to make known to the sons of men Thy mighty deeds,
and the glorious splendor of Thy kingdom.
Thy kingdom is an everlasting kingdom,
and Thy dominion endures throughout all generations.

(Ps 145.1–3, 10–13)

The prophets called all of the earthly kings, the "shepherds of Israel," to repentance before the divine King of heaven, but their words were mostly to no avail.

The word of the Lord came to me: "Son of man, prophesy against the
shepherds of Israel, prophesy, and say to them, even to the shepherds,
Thus says the Lord God: Ho, shepherds of Israel who have been feeding
yourselves! Should not shepherds feed the sheep? You eat the fat, you
clothe yourselves with the wool, you slaughter the fatlings; but you do
not feed the sheep. The weak you have not strengthened, the sick you
have not healed, the crippled you have not bound up, the strayed you
have not brought back, the lost you have not sought, and with force
and harshness you have ruled them. So they were scattered, because
there was no shepherd; and they became food for all the wild beasts.
My sheep were scattered over all the mountains and on every high
hill; my sheep were scattered over all the face of the earth, with none
to search or seek for them" (Ezek 34.1–6).

The psalms and the prophets of the Old Testament also foretold the time when God would rule His People directly. He would be the shepherd of all nations, ruling through the Messiah-King Who would come from the house of David, the King of Whose kingdom there would be no end.

For to us a child is born,
to us a son is given;
and the government will be upon His shoulder,
and His name will be called
"Wonderful Counselor, Mighty God,
Everlasting Father, Prince of Peace."
Of the increase of His government and of peace there will be no end,
upon the throne of David, and over His kingdom,
to establish it, and to uphold it
with justice and with righteousness
from this time forth and for evermore.
The zeal of the Lord of hosts will do this (Is 4.6–7).

"Behold, the days are coming, says the Lord, when I will raise up for David a righteous Branch, and He shall reign as king and deal wisely, and shall execute justice and righteousness in the land. In His days Judah will be saved, and Israel will dwell securely. And this is the name by which He will be called: 'The Lord is our righteousness'" (Jer 23.5–6).

But you, O Bethlehem Ephrathah,
who are little to be among the clans of Judah,
from you shall come forth for me
one is to be ruler in Israel,
whose origin is from of old,
from ancient days.
Therefore he shall give them up until the time

when she who is in travail has brought forth;
then the rest of his brethren shall return
to the people of Israel.
And He shall stand and feed His flock
in the strength of the Lord,
in the majesty of the name of the Lord his God.
And they shall dwell secure, for now
He shall be great
to the ends of the earth (Mic 5.2–4)

For thus says the Lord God: Behold, I, I myself will search for my sheep,
and will seek them out. As a shepherd seeks out his flock when some of
his sheep have been scattered abroad, so will I seek out my sheep; and
I will rescue them from all places where they have been scattered on a
day of clouds and thick darkness.

I myself will be the shepherd of my sheep, and I will make them
lie down, says the Lord God. I will seek the lost, and I will bring back
the strayed, and I will bind up the crippled, and I will strengthen the
weak, and the fat and the strong I will watch over; I will feed them
in justice (Ezek 34.11–12, 15–16).

Rejoice greatly, O daughter of Zion!
Shout aloud, O daughter of Jerusalem!
Lo, your king comes to you;
triumphant and victorious is he,
humble and riding on an ass,
on a colt the foal of an ass.
I will cut off the chariot from Ephraim
and the war horse from Jerusalem;
and the battle bow shall be cut off,
and He shall command peace to the nations;
His dominion shall be from sea to sea,
and from the River to the ends of the earth (Zech 9.9–10).

The king of the final kingdom of God is Jesus Christ. He is the One Shepherd and Lord. He is the One "of whose kingdom there will be no end." Thus, the angel Gabriel speaks to Mary at the announcement of His birth:

He will be great, and will be called the Son of the Most High; and the Lord God will give to Him the throne of His father David, and He will reign over the house of Jacob for ever; and of His kingdom there will be no end" (Lk 1.32–33).

All of His life, Jesus was preparing the everlasting Kingdom of God. He came to bring this Kingdom to men. He is the Son of David, Who will reign forever. He is the One Who announces the gospel of the Kingdom of God (Mt 4.23, 9.35).

Being asked by the Pharisees when the kingdom of God was coming, He answered them, "The kingdom of God is not coming with signs to be observed; nor will they say, 'Lo, here it is!' or 'There!' for behold, the kingdom of God is in the midst of you" (Lk 17.20–21).

The Kingdom of God is in the midst of men when Christ is present. He Himself is the King Who gives the Kingdom of God to those who are this.

Fear not, little flock, for it is your Father's good pleasure to give you the kingdom" (Lk 12.32).

You are those who have continued with me in my trials; as my Father appointed a kingdom for me, so do I appoint for you that you may eat and drink at my table in my kingdom . . . (Lk 22.28–30).

All of the preaching and parables of Christ concerning the Kingdom of God speak of Himself as the King. Those who believe in Jesus and obey Him will reign with Him in His Kingdom which has been prepared "from the foundation of the world" for those who love Him

(Mt 25.34). His Kingdom is the everlasting kingdom which is "not of this world," but of God the Father (Jn 18.36).

The gospel narratives of the crucifixion of Christ place Him in His role as King, All of the mockery and torment of Jesus is given to Him as the "King of the Jews." This was the accusation against Him and the title nailed to the cross. Thus, the irony is complete as the scriptures are fulfilled in the words of Pilate when, after Jesus had sat down on the judgment seat, Pilate proclaimed to the people, "Behold, your king!" (Jn 19.14).

Jesus is the King. He is one with God, the "King of kings and Lord of lords" (1 Tim 6.5). He is the One "highly exalted" over all principalities and powers, the One before Whom every knee shall bow "In heaven, and on earth and under the earth" (Phil 2.9–11, also Eph 1.20–23). He is the One Who, at the end of the ages when He "comes in His kingdom" with all the heavenly powers, will destroy every evil, and rule over all creation forever as the prophets predicted.

> . . . and the Lamb (Christ) will conquer them [the wicked], for He is Lord of lords and King of kings, and those with Him are called and chosen and faithful (Rev 17.14).

> Then I saw heaven opened, and behold, a white horse! He who sat upon it is called Faithful and True, and in righteousness He judges and makes war. His eyes are like a flame of fire, and on His head are many diadems; and He has a name inscribed which no one knows but Himself. He is clad in a robe dipped in blood, and the name by which He is called is The Word of God. And the armies of heaven, arrayed in fine linen, white and pure, followed Him on white horses. From His mouth issues a sharp sword with which to smite the nations, and He will rule them with a rod of iron He will tread the wine press of the fury of the wrath of God the Almighty. On His robe and on His thigh He has a name inscribed, King of kings and Lord of lords (Rev 19.11–16).

Then He showed me the river of the water of Life, bright as crystal, flowing from the throne of God and of the Lamb through the middle of the street of the city; also, on either side of the river, the tree of life with its twelve kinds of fruit, yielding its fruit each month; and the leaves of the tree were for the healing of the nations. There shall no more be anything accursed, but the throne of God and of the Lamb shall be in it, and His servants shall worship Him; they shall see His face, and His name shall be on their foreheads. And night shall be no more; they need no light of lamp or sun, for the Lord God will be their light, and they shall reign for ever and ever (Rev 22.1–5).

Priesthood

When speaking of Abraham, we mentioned how Jesus Christ is the "priest forever according to the order of Melchizedek." As the "priest for ever," Jesus is also the completion and fulfillment of the Old Testament priesthood of the Levites.

In the Old Testament, God ordered Moses to build the tabernacle with a sanctuary for worship and sacrifice.

And let them make me a sanctuary, that I may dwell in their midst, According to all that I show you concerning the tabernacle, and all of its furniture, so you shall make it (Ex 25.8–9).

In the tabernacle there was a sanctuary surrounded by a court yard. Within the sanctuary was the "most holy place." A special ark was built to hold the tables of the covenant law surrounded by two cherubim. The ark was kept in the most holy place. Above the ark of the covenant was the mercy seat from which Moses would speak to the people (Ex 25.14–22).

In the sanctuary, special tables were placed which held "plates and dishes for incense" and "flagons and bowls with which to pour libations."

. . .of pure gold you shall make them. And you shall set the bread of the Presence on the table before me always (Ex 25.28–30).

There also was the golden altar upon which the animal sacrifices were offered.

A lampstand of gold, with "seven lamps for it" which were lighted with pure olive oil, was placed in the sanctuary. And between the various part of the tabernacle, curtains were hung.

"And you shall make a veil of blue and purple and scarlet stuff and fine twined linen; in skilled work shall it be made, with cherubim; and you shall hang it upon four pillars of acacia overlaid with gold, with hooks of gold, upon four bases of silver. And you shall hang the veil from the clasps, and bring the ark of the testimony in thither within the veil; and the veil shall separate for you the holy place from the most holy. You shall put the mercy seat upon the ark of the testimony in the most holy place. And you shall set the table outside the veil, and the lampstand on the south side of the tabernacle opposite the table; and you shall put the table on the north side. And you shall make a screen for the door of the tent, of blue and purple and scarlet stuff and fine twined linen, embroidered with needlework. And you shall make for the screen five pillars of acacia, and overlay them with gold; their hooks shall be of gold, and you shall cast five bases of bronze for them. You shall make the altar of acacia wood, five cubits long and five cubits broad; the altar shall be a square, and its height shall be three cubits. And you shall make horns for it on its four corners; its horns shall be of one piece with it, and you shall overlay it with bronze (Ex 26.31–27.2).

The priests of the tabernacle were to be the Levites, the men from the tribe of Levi.

Then bring near to you Aaron your brother, and his sons with him, from among the people of Israel, to serve me as priests . . . (Ex 28.1)

God commanded that special vestments be made for the priests to wear when serving in the sanctuary (Ex 28). He also ordered that special oil be blended for the anointing of all of the utensils of the tabernacle, as well as for the anointing of the priests. He also ordered special incense to be made for burning in the holy place.

> *. . . you shall consecrate them [the furniture and utensils], that they may be holy; whatever touches them will become holy. And you shall anoint Aaron and his sons, and consecrate them, that they may serve me as priests. And you shall say to the people of Israel, 'This is my holy anointing oil throughout your generations.' (Ex 30.29–31)*

> *And the incense which you shall make according to its composition, you shall not make for yourselves; it shall be for you holy to the Lord* (Ex 30.37).

God also provided a very detailed code concerning worship and the offering of the various sacrifices. He explained which animals should be selected and how they should be killed. He told which offerings should be made on which occasions and for what purposes. He gave instructions about offerings for peace and for praise, for thanksgiving and mercy, for forgiveness of sins and reconciliation with God in times of transgression. He also told which feasts should be observed, when they should be kept and how they should be celebrated, The books of **Exodus, Leviticus, Numbers**, and **Deuteronomy** are filled with such specific and detailed instructions.

While passing through the desert and into the promised land, the People of God carried the tabernacle with them. They set it up in each place where they camped. Finally, after the crossing of the Jordan River and the settlement in Canaan, the city of Jerusalem was established by David the king. David's son Solomon was then commanded by God to build the temple in which the worship of God would take place and the ritual sacrifices would be offered.

In the four hundred and eightieth year after the people of Israel came out of the land of Egypt, in the fourth year of Solomon's reign over Israel . . . he began to build the house of the Lord (1 Kg 6.1).

The house of the Lord was of the same pattern as Moses' tabernacle. It had the outer court, the inner sanctuary and the most holy place in which the ark of the covenant was kept. It had the altars for incense, libations and burnt offerings. It had the lampstands and the table for the bread of the Presence. It had all of the utensils and vestments necessary for the service of the Lord (see 1 Kg 6–8).

When Solomon finished building the temple (c. 960 BC), he conducted a great celebration of dedication.

> *Then the priests brought the ark of the covenant of the Lord to its place, in the inner sanctuary of the house, in the most holy place, underneath the wings of the cherubim.*
>
> *There was nothing in the ark except the two tab lets of stone, which Moses put there at Horeb, where the Lord made a covenant with the people of Israel, when He brought them out of the land of Egypt. And when the priests came out of the holy place, a cloud filled the house of the Lord, so that the priests could not stand to minister because of the cloud; for the glory of the Lord filled the house of the Lord. Then Solomon said, "The Lord has set the sun in the heavens, but has said that He would dwell in thick darkness. I have built thee an exalted house, a place for thee to dwell in for ever"* (1 Kg 8.6, 9–13).

Solomon then blessed the people and addressed them concerning the building of the temple which the Lord promised David that his son would build. He then offered a long prayer of dedication, asking God to be with the people and to receive their prayers offered in the temple.

> *"But will God indeed dwell on the earth? Behold, heaven and the highest heaven cannot contain thee; how much less this house which I have built! Yet have regard to the prayer of thy servant and to his supplication, O Lord my God, hearkening to the cry and to the prayer which Thy servant prays before Thee this day; that Thine eyes may be open night and day toward this house, the place of which Thou hast said, 'My name shall be there,' that Thou mayest hearken to the prayer which Thy servant offers toward this place. And hearken Thou to the supplication of Thy servant and of Thy people Israel, when they pray toward this place; yea, hear Thou in heaven Thy dwelling place; and when Thou hearest, forgive"* (1 Kg 8.27–30).

Thus, the temple which Solomon built to the Lord became the sole place for the formal worship and the priestly sacrifices of the People of God. The temple was destroyed during the time of Babylonian captivity, and was restored in the time of Ezra and Nehemiah only to be defiled again by foreign invaders, and finally destroyed completely by the Romans in the year 70 AD.

It was prophesied in the Old Testament that the time would come when the glory of the Lord would fill all creation. It was foretold that in the time of the Messianic King, God would dwell in men as in His holy temple. The ritual sacrifices of the temple would cease, as the perfect and everlasting covenant of mercy and peace would be accomplished between God and man (see Isa 55.3, 61.1–11, 66.18–23, Jer 31.31–34. Ezek 34.22–31, 37.24–28).

When Jesus came, the new and everlasting covenant between God and man was established forever. The temple of God became the body of Christ, which was the assembly of His people filled with the Holy Spirit of God. Indeed, one of the accusations against Jesus at the time of His crucifixion was that He said that He would destroy the temple in Jerusalem.

The Passover of the Jews was at hand, and Jesus went up to Jerusalem. In the temple He found those who were selling oxen and sheep and pigeons, and the money-changers at their business. And making a whip of cords, He drove them all, with the sheep and oxen, out of the temple; and He poured out the coins of the money-changers and overturned their tables. And Ne told those who sold the pigeons, "Take these things away; you shall not make my Father's house a house of trade." His disciples remembered that it was written, "Zeal for thy house will consume me." The Jews then said to Him, "What sign have you to show us for doing this?" Jesus answered them, "Destroy this temple, and in three days I will raise it up." The Jews then said, "It has taken forty-six years to build this temple, and will you raise it up in three days?" But He spoke of the temple of His body. When therefore He was raised from the dead, His disciples remembered that He had said this; and they believed the scripture and the word which Jesus had spoken (Jn 2.13–22).

Now the chief priests and the whole council sought false testimony against Jesus that they might put Him to death, but they found none, though many false witnesses came forward. At last two came forward and said, "This fellow said, 'I am able to destroy the temple of God, and to build it in three days.'" And the high priest stood up and said, "Have you no answer to make? What is it that these men testify against you?" But Jesus was silent. And the high priest said to Him, "I adjure you by the living God, tell us if you are the Christ, the Son of God." Jesus said to him, "You have said so. But I tell you, hereafter you will see the Son of man seated at the right hand of Power, and coming on the clouds of heaven" (Mt 26.59–64).

In Christ, the Messiah, human persons become the temple of the Living God. The deacon Stephen, the first Christian martyr, bore witness to this and died for his testimony (see Acts 7.44–59). The apostle Paul also taught this explicitly, as did the apostle Peter.

But now in Christ Jesus you who once were far off have been brought near in the blood of Christ. For He is our peace, who has made us both one, and has broken down the dividing wall of hostility, by abolishing in His flesh the law of commandments and ordinances, that He might create in Himself one new man in place of two, so making peace, and might reconcile us both to God in one body through the cross, thereby bringing the hostility to an end. And He came and preached peace to you who were far off and peace to those who were near; for through Him we both have access in one Spirit to the Father. So then you are no longer strangers and sojourners, but you are fellow citizens with the saints and members of the household of God, built upon the foundation of the apostles and prophets, Christ Jesus Himself being the cornerstone, in whom the whole structure is joined together and grows into a holy temple in the Lord; in whom you also are built into it for a dwelling place of God in the Spirit (Eph 2.13–22).

Do you not know that you are God's temple and that God's Spirit dwells in you? If any one destroys God's temple, God will destroy him. For God's temple is holy, and that temple you are (1 Cor 3.16–17).

Come to Him, to that living stone, rejected by men but in God's sight chosen and precious; and like living stones be yourselves built into a spiritual house, to be a holy priesthood, to offer spiritual sacrifices acceptable to God through Jesus Christ. For it stands in scripture: "Behold, I am laying in Zion a stone, a cornerstone chosen and precious, and he who believes in Him will not be put to shame" (1 Pet 2.4–6).

Jesus Christ is not only the **living temple** of God—God Himself in human flesh—through whom all men become God's temple in the Holy Spirit; Jesus is also the one great **high priest** and the one perfect **sacrificial offering,** Who assumes and fulfills the entire Levitical priesthood of the Old Testament which was merely a "shadow" of the "reality" to come. Upon the cross, Jesus sacrificed Himself. He rose from the dead and entered the sanctuary in heaven. After this, there is no other priesthood and no other sacrifice well-pleasing to God (see Heb 6–10).

> But when Christ appeared as a high priest of the good things that have come, then through the greater and more perfect tabernacle (not made with hands, that is, not of this creation) He entered once for all into the Holy place, taking not the blood of goats and calves but His own blood, thus securing an eternal redemption. For if the sprinkling of defiled persons with the blood of goats and bulls and with the ashes of a heifer sanctifies for the purification of the flesh, how much more shall the blood of Christ, who through the eternal Spirit offered Himself without blemish to God, purify your conscience from dead works to serve the living God (Heb 9.11–14).

> For Christ has entered, not into a sanctuary made with hands, a copy of the true one, but into heaven itself, now to appear in the presence of God on our behalf. Nor was it to offer Himself repeatedly, as the high priest enters the Holy Place yearly with blood not his own; for then He would have had to suffer repeatedly since the foundation of the world. But as it is, He has appeared once for all at the end of the age to put away sin by the sacrifice of Himself. And just as it is appointed for men to die once, and after that comes judgment, so Christ, having been offered once to bear the sins of many, will appear a second time, not to deal with sin, but to save those who are eagerly waiting for Hint (Heb 9.24–28).

Consequently, when Christ came into die world, He said, "Sacrifices and offerings thou hast not desired, but a body h ast thou prepared for me; in burnt offerings and sin offerings thou hast taken no pleasure. Then I said, 'lo, I have come to do thy will, O God,' as it is written of me in the roll of the book." When He said above, "Thou hast neither desired nor taken pleasure in sacrifices and offerings and burnt offerings and sin offerings" (these are offered according to the law), then He added, "Lo, I have come to do thy will." He abolishes the first in order to establish the second. And by that will we have been sanctified through the offering of the body of Jesus Christ once for all. And every priest stands daily at His service, offering repeatedly the same sacrifices, which can never take away sins. But when Christ had offered for all time a single sacrifice for sins, He sat down at the right hand of God, then to wait until His enemies should be made a stool for His feet. For by a single offering He has perfected for all time those who are sanctified (Heb 10.5–14).

In the Church of Christ, there is only one priesthood and one sacrifice. It is the priesthood of Jesus and the sacrifice of the Cross. The entire Church of Christ is a "royal priesthood" (1 Pet 2.4). The ordained clergy of the Church exists to manifest and realize the unique priesthood of Jesus in the community which is the "body of Christ" (1 Cor 12.27).

In the Kingdom of God, Christ, the great High Priest and Lamb will rule. He Who "was dead and is alive again" (Rev 2.8) will govern all creation which will be the dwelling place of God.

And I saw no temple in the heavenly city, for its temple is the Lord God the Almighty and the Lamb. And the city has no need of sun or moon to shine upon it, for the glory of God is its light, and its lamp is the Lamb. By its light shall the nations walk; and the kings of the earth shall bring their glory into it, and its gates shall never be shut by day—and there shall be no night there; they shall bring into it the glory and the honor of the nations. But nothing unclean shall enter it, nor any one who practices abomination or falsehood, but only those who are written in the Lamb's book of life (Rev 21.22–27).

Thus, the Old Testament temple, the priesthood and the sacrifices are all fulfilled in Christ Who is Himself the Temple and the Priest and the Sacrificed Lamb of the Kingdom of God which exists for His People whom He has made "a kingdom, priests to His God and Father" (Rev 1.16, 6.10).

Prophecy

The Old Testament is filled with prophecy. Prophecy means the direct inspiration of God to speak His words to the world. There were many prophets in the Old Testament, not only those whose names are given to the prophetic books of the Bible, but many others, including Moses, Elijah, Samuel and Nathan.

In the Old Testament, many prophecies were made concerning the history and destiny of the people of Israel and of the whole human race. Usually the prophecies told what God would do in response to the wickedness and unfaithfulness of His People. The prophecies foretold the tragedies coming to Israel because of the sins of the People. They also foretold the ultimate mercy and forgiveness of God Who is faithful to His promises, Who will not be angry forever, but Who will restore the fortunes of His People and bring all nations to His everlasting Kingdom.

The ultimate act of God's mercy and compassion is His sending of His Son as the Messiah of Israel. Jesus, as we have seen, is the final King of God's Kingdom which reigns forever. He is the great high priest Who brings completion and perfection to man's priestly sacrifices to God. He is also the last and final Prophet Who ushers in the time when God creates a whole people of prophets, a whole assembly of those who are taught directly by God to know His Will and to speak His Words in the world.

Thus, in the Gospel of Saint John, it is recorded that the people recognized Jesus not merely as a prophet or one of the prophets, but as the final Prophet Whom God would send at the end of the ages.

> *When the people saw the sign which He had done [the feeding of the five thousand], they said, "This is indeed the Prophet Who is come into the world!"* (Jn 6.14)

> *When they heard these words (about the living water), some of the people said, "This is really the Prophet." Others said, "This is the Christ"* (Jn 7.40).

Saint Peter refers to the same appearance of Christ as the Prophet, in his preaching to the people outside the temple in Jerusalem.

> *Moses said, "The Lord God will raise up for you a prophet from your brethren as He raised me up. You shall listen to Him in whatever He tells you. And it shall be that every soul that does not listen to that prophet shall be destroyed from the people"* (Acts 3.22–23).

Jesus is "that prophet" whom Moses spoke about in the Old Law (Dt 18.15). But even Moses and all the prophets of old did not realize that "that prophet" would be the divine Son and the uncreated Word of God in human flesh.

Jesus, as the final Prophet, is more than a prophet. He is radically different from the prophets of old. He is the "teacher come from God" (Jn 3.2), Who "speaks as one having authority" (Mt 7.24, Mk 1.22), Who speaks not His own words, but the words of the Father Who sent Him (Jn 14: 24). But He is even more than this because He is Himself the divine Word of' God in human flesh.

> *In the beginning was the Word, and the Word was with God, and the Word was God. He was in the beginning with God; all things*

were made through Him, and without Him was not anything made that was made. In Him was life, and the life was the light of men (Jn 1.1–4).

And the Word became flesh and dwelt among us, full of grace and truth; we have beheld His glory, glory as of the only Son from the Father (Jn 1.14).

And from His fulness have we all received, grace upon grace. For the law was given through Moses; grace and truth came through Jesus Christ. No one has ever seen God; the only Son who is in the bosom of the Father, He has made Him known (Jn 1.16–18).

As the Word of God in human flesh, Jesus fulfills the prophecy of the great prophets of old who wrote that in the Messiah's time, all men would be taught directly by God.

> *For a brief moment I forsook you,*
> *but with great compassion I will gather you.*
> *In overflowing wrath for a moment I hid my face from you,*
> *but with everlasting love I will have compassion on you,*
> *says the Lord, your Redeemer.*
> *For the mountains may depart and the hills be removed,*
> *but my steadfast love shall not depart from you,*
> *and my covenant of peace shall not be removed,*
> *says the Lord, who has compassion on you.*
> *All your sons shall be taught by the Lord,*
> *And great shall be the prosperity of your sons.*
> *In righteousness you shall be established;*
> *you shall be far from oppression, for you shall not fear;*
> *and from terror, for it shall not come near you*
>
> (Is 54.7–8, 10, 13–14).

But this is the covenant which I will make with the house of Israel after those days, says the Lord: I will put my law within them, and I will write it upon their hearts; and I will be their God, and they shall be my people. And no longer shall each man teach his neighbor and each his brother, saying 'Know the Lord,' for they shall all know me, from the least of them to the greatest, says the Lord; for I will forgive their iniquity, and I will remember their sin no more (Jer 31.33–34).

As the Prophet and the incarnate Word of God, Jesus is the Way, the Truth, the Life, and the Light of the world.

Jesus said to him, "I am the way, and the truth, and the life; no one comes to the Father, but by me. If you had known me, you would have known my Father also; henceforth you know Him and have seen Him" (Jn 14.6–7).

Again Jesus spoke to them, saying, "I am the light of the world; he who follows me will not walk in darkness, but will have the light of life" (Jn 8.12).

Jesus shares His gift of prophecy with all who belong to Him. He gives the Holy Spirit to all of His disciples that they too might know the Father and speak His words and be themselves "the light of the world."

You are the light of the world. A city set on a hill cannot be hid. Nor do men light a lamp and put it under a bushel, but on a stand, and it gives light to all in the house. Let your light so shine before men, that they may see your good works and give glory to your Father who is in heaven (Mt 5.14–16).

. . . and you will be dragged before governors and kings for my sake, to bear testimony before them and the Gentiles. When they deliver you up, do not be anxious how you are to speak or what you are to

say; for what you are to say will be given to you in that hour; for it is not you who speak, but the Spirit of your Father speaking through you (Mt 10.18–20).

The full possibility for men to prophesy is given in the gift of the Holy Spirit Who came to Christ's disciples on Pentecost and continues to come upon all who in the Church are baptized into Christ. This full outpouring of the Spirit of God on all flesh was itself prophesied by Joel in the Old Testament. Thus once again, the apostle Peter bears witness:

But Peter, standing with the eleven, lifted up his voice and addressed them, "Men of Judea and all who dwell in Jerusalem, let this be known to you, and give ear to my words. For these men are not drunk, as you suppose, since it is only the third hour of the day: but this is what was spoken by the prophet Joel:

'And in the last days it shall be, God declares,
that I will pour out my Spirit upon all flesh,
and your sons and your daughters shall prophesy,
and your young men shall see visions,
and your old men shall dream dreams;
yea, and on my menservants and my maidservants in those days
I will pour out my Spirit; and they shall prophesy.'

(Acts 2.14–18)

The apostle Paul concurs with Peter as he insists that prophecy is the first of the gifts of the Holy Spirit in the Church of the Messiah.

Make love your aim, and earnestly desire the spiritual gifts, especially that you may prophesy (1 Cor 14.1).

In the Kingdom of God, all prophecy will cease, for the final and perfect presence of God will be given. Then Christ, the Word of God, will be present in all of His divine glory, manifesting God the Father to the whole of creation.

Holiness

The God of the Old Testament was the Holy God. The word **holy** means separate, different, unlike anything else that exists.

The Holy God of the Old Testament revealed Himself to His chosen people who were able to behold His glory. The **glory** of the Lord was a special divine manifestation of the Person and Presence of God. It consisted in the vision of light, majesty and beauty and was accompanied by the voice of the Lord and His holy angels. It created in the persons who observed it overwhelming feelings of fear and fascination, as well as profound convictions of peace, well-being, and joy.

In this way did Moses experience the Holy God in His divine glory on Horeb, the mountain of God., before the passover, and in the wilderness after the exodus from Egypt.

And the angel of the Lord appeared to him in a flame of fire out of the midst of a bush; and he looked, and to, the bush was burning, yet it was not consumed. And Moses said, "I will turn aside and see this great sight, why the bush is not burnt." When the Lord saw that he turned aside to see, God called to him out of the bush, "Moses, Moses!" And He said, "Here am I." Then He said, "Do not come near; put off your shoes from your feet, for the place on which you are standing is holy ground." And He said, "I am the God of your father, the God of Abraham, the God of Isaac, and tile God of Jacob." And Moses hid his face, for he was afraid to look at God (Ex 3.2–6).

Moses said, "I pray thee, show me thy glory." And He said, "I will make all my goodness pass before you, and will proclaim before you my name 'The Lord'; and I will be gracious to whom I will be gracious, and will show mercy on whom I will show mercy. "But," he said, "you cannot see my face; for man shall not see me and live." And the Lord said, "Behold, there is a place by me where you shall stand upon the rock; and while my glory passes by I will put you in a cleft of the rock, and I will cover you with my hand until I have passed by; then I will take away my hand, and you shall see my back; but my face shall not be seen" (Ex 33.18–23).

Other select persons of the Old Testament also experienced the presence of divine holiness and the glory of God. Abraham, Isaac, Jacob, Elijah, and Ezekiel had such experiences, as did Isaiah whose classic vision has become a standard part of the Church's liturgical prayer.

In the year that King Uzziah died, I saw the Lord sitting upon a throne, high and lifted up, and His train filled the temple. Above Him stood the seraphim; each had six wings: with two he covered his face, and with two he covered his feet, and with two he flew. And one called to another and said:

"Holy, holy, holy is the Lord of hosts;
and the whole earth is full of his glory."

And the foundations of the thresholds shook at the voice of him who
called, and the house was filled with smoke, And I said: "Woe is me!
For I am lost; for I am a man of unclean lips, and I dwell in the midst
of a people of unclean lips; for my eyes have seen the King, the Lord
of hosts!" Then flew one of the seraphim to me, having in his hand a
burning coal which he had taken with tongs from the altar. And he
touched my mouth, and said: "Behold, this has touched your lips; your
guilt is taken away, and your sin forgiven." And I heard the voice of
the Lord saying, "Whom shall I send, and who will go for us?" Then
I said, "Here am I! Send me."

(Is 6.1–8)

The psalms also sing of the holiness of God and proclaim that all
creation speaks of God's glory (see Ps 8, 19, 93, 104, 148, et al.).

The main teaching of the Old Testament and the foundation of
all of its life was that God's people should share in His holiness. This
was the purpose of the entire Law of Moses in its commandments of
morality and worship.

For I am the Lord your God; consecrate yourselves therefore, and be
holy, for I am holy. You shall not defile yourselves with any swarming
thing that crawls upon the earth. For I am the Lord who brought you
up out of the land of Egypt, to be your God; you shall therefore be holy,
for I am holy (Lev 11.44–45).

The people were to be holy and to gain the wisdom and righteousness of God through their service and worship of Him. All of the so-
called Wisdom writings of the Old Testament, and all of the teachings
of the prophets and psalms are centered around this same fundamental
fact: God's people should acquire and express the holiness, wisdom,

glory, and righteousness of God Himself. This, and nothing else is the meaning and purpose of man's life as created and guided by God.

The ultimate perfection of God's purpose for man is fulfilled in Christ. He alone is the fulfillment of the law and the prophets. He alone is the "Holy One of God" (Mk 1.24, Lk 1.35, 4.34). He alone is perfectly righteous and wholly without sin. Thus, St Peter speaks of Jesus to the people after the event of Pentecost.

> *The God of Abraham and of Isaac and of Jacob, the God of our fathers, glorified His servant Jesus, whom you delivered up and denied in the presence of Pilate, when he had decided to release Him. But you denied the Holy and Righteous One, and asked for a murderer to be granted to you, and killed the Author of life, whom God raised from the dead. To this we are witnesses* (Acts 3.13–15).

The apostle Paul concurs with the teaching of Peter by referring to Christ not merely as holy, righteous and wise, but as Himself the very holiness, righteousness and wisdom of God Himself in human flesh.

> *For Jews demand signs and Greeks seek wisdom, but we preach Christ crucified, a stumbling block to Jews and folly to Gentiles, but to those who are called, both Jews and Greeks, Christ the power of God and the wisdom of God.*
>
> *He is the source of your life in Christ Jesus, whom God made our wisdom, our righteousness, and sanctification and redemption; therefore, as it is written, "Let him who boasts, boast of the Lord"* (1 Cor 1.22–24, 30–31).

The glory of God is revealed in the person of Christ. This is the consistent witness of the apostles who beheld the "Kingdom of God come with power" on the mountain of the Transfiguration (see Mt 17.1–6, Mk 9.2–7, Lk 9.28–36).

And the Word became flesh and dwelt among us, full of grace and truth; we have beheld His glory, glory as of the only Son from the Father (Jn 1.14).

Now if the dispensation of death, carved in letters on stone, came with such splendor that the Israelites could not look at Moses' face because of its brightness, fading as this was, will not the dispensation of the Spirit be attended with greater splendor? For if there was splendor in the dispensation of condemnation, the dispensation of righteousness must far exceed it in splendor. Indeed, in this case, what once had splendor has come to have no splendor at all, because of the splendor that surpasses it. For if what faded away came with splendor, what is permanent must have much more splendor. Since we have such a hope, we are very bold.

And we all, with unveiled face, beholding the glory of the Lord, are being changed into His likeness from one degree of glory to another; for this comes from the Lord who is the Spirit.

For it is the God who said, "Let light shine out of darkness," who has shone in our hearts to give the light of the knowledge of the glory of God in the face of Christ (2 Cor 3.7, 18, 4.6).

In and through Christ, by means of the Holy Spirit, all men can share in the glory of God and become participants in God's own holiness.

His divine power has granted to us all things that pertain to life and godliness, through the knowledge of Him who called us to His glory and excellence, by which He has granted to us His precious and very great promises, that through these you may escape from the corruption that is in the world because of passion, and become partakers of the divine nature (2 Pet 1.3–4).

The participation of men in the "nature of God" already begins in the Church of Christ, the final fruit of the salvation history of the Old

Testament. In the Church, the Kingdom of God is present which is "righteousness and peace and joy in the Holy Spirit" (Rom 14.17). In the Church of Christ already begins that perpetual praise of the Holy God which exists now in the heavens and will fill all creation when Christ comes in the glory of His Kingdom at the end of the ages.

Holy, holy, holy, is the Lord God Almighty,
who was and is to come! (Rev 4.8b).

And he said to me, "These words are trustworthy and true. And the Lord, the God of the spirits of the prophets, has sent His angel to show His servants what must soon take place. And behold, I am coming soon." Blessed is he who keeps the words of the prophecy of this book (Rev 22.6–7).

Let the evildoer still do evil, and the filthy still be filthy, and the righteous still do right, and the holy still be holy. Behold, I am coming soon, bringing my recompense, to repay every one for what he has done. I am the Alpha and the Omega, the first and the last, the beginning and the end. Blessed are those who wash their robes, that they may have the right to the tree of life and that they may enter the city by the gates. Outside are the dogs and sorcerers and fornicators and murderers and idolaters, and every one who loves and practices falsehood. I Jesus have sent my angel to you with this testimony for the churches. I am the root and the offspring of David, the bright morning star (Rev 22.11–16).

He who testifies to these things says, "Surely I am coming soon." Amen. Come, Lord Jesus! The grace of the Lord be with all the saints. Amen (Rev 22.20–21)

We hope this book has been enjoyable and edifying for your spiritual journey toward our Lord and Savior Jesus Christ.

One hundred percent of the net proceeds of all SVS Press sales directly support the mission of St Vladimir's Orthodox Theological Seminary to train priests, lay leaders, and scholars to be active apologists of the Orthodox Christian Faith. However, the proceeds only partially cover the operational costs of St Vladimir's Seminary. To meet our annual budget, we rely on the generosity of donors who are passionate about providing theological education and spiritual formation to the next generation of ordained and lay servant leaders in the Orthodox Church.

 Donations are tax-deductible and can be made at www.svots.edu/donate. We greatly appreciate your generosity.

To engage more with St Vladimir's Orthodox Theological Seminary, please visit:

www.svots.edu
online.svots.edu
www.svspress.com
www.instituteofsacredarts.com

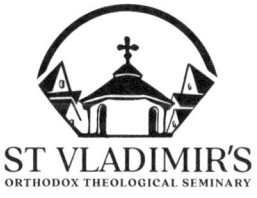